GLOBALVIEWPOINTS

Extreme Weather
Events

Other Books of Related Interest

At Issue Series

Adaptation and Climate Change
Are Natural Disasters Increasing?
Is Global Warming a Threat?
Should There Be an International Climate Treaty?

Confronting Global Warming Series

Extreme Weather
Population, Resources and Conflict
The Role of the Government
The Role of the Individual

Global Viewpoints Series

Climate Change
Disasters

Opposing Viewpoints Series

Global Warming
Natural Disasters

GLOBALVIEWPOINTS

Extreme Weather Events

Marcia Amidon Lusted, Book Editor

GREENHAVEN
PUBLISHING

Published in 2018 by Greenhaven Publishing, LLC
353 3rd Avenue, Suite 255, New York, NY 10010

Copyright © 2018 by Greenhaven Publishing, LLC

First Edition

Cover image: Todd Shoemake/Shutterstock.com
Map: frees/Shutterstock.com

Library of Congress Cataloging-in-Publication Data

Names: Lusted, Marcia Amidon, editor.
Title: Extreme weather events / edited by Marcia Amidon Lusted.
Description: New York : Greenhaven Publishing, 2018. | Series: Global viewpoints | Includes
  bibliographical references and index. | Audience: Grades 9-12.
Identifiers: LCCN ISBN 9781534501140 (library bound) | ISBN 9781534501126 (pbk.)
Subjects: LCSH: Climatic extremes. | Weather--Environmental aspects. |
Climatic changes—Health aspects. | Weather—Health aspects.
Classification: LCC QC981.8.C53 E94 2018 | DDC 551.55—dc23

Manufactured in the United States of America

Website: http://greenhavenpublishing.com

Contents

Foreword   **9**

Introduction   **12**

Chapter 1: Extreme Weather Around the World

1. The Global Links Between Extreme Weather and   **17**
Climate Change
Daniel Huber and Jay Gulledge
While climate change is usually discussed in terms
of changing temperatures and precipitation, it is the
increasingly extreme and severe weather events that will
create the biggest social and economic costs.

2. The Atlantic Ocean Brings a Wave of Climate   **35**
Change
United Nations Environment Programme
This report, sponsored by the UNEP, explains how the
oceans can influence the earth's climate, both in the long
term and the short term. Ocean currents and temperatures
are one of the biggest factors in climate variation.

3. Climate Change and Global Warming 101   **40**
Anup Shah
There are some common questions about climate change
and global warming, greenhouse gases, and the carbon
cycle, as well as how extreme weather events are related to
climate change.

4. Coastal Resilience Is Key for the US and the World   **56**
Erin A. Thead
The change in sea levels is one of the most important
indicators of climate change. Rising sea levels will impact
many cities across the world, and they must plan for the
effects on their inhabitants.

5. In the US, Hurricanes Are a Harbinger of Climate   **64**
Doom
John McQuaid

Because of changing global temperatures, hurricanes are increasing in severity. Observation and modeling are essential to help predict when these more dangerous storms are going to occur.

6. Weird Weather Around the World Is Cause for Alarm   71
   Christine Ottery
   Extreme, or "weird," weather incidents seem to be increasing. Are they related to climate change?

Periodical and Internet Sources Bibliography   78

Chapter 2: The Effects of Extreme Weather

1. Climate Has an Impact on Global Health   81
   US Environmental Protection Agency
   The EPA explains the specific ways in which humans will be impacted by changing climate conditions and extreme weather.

2. Animal Populations Are Affected by Climate Upheaval   93
   Juan Lubroth
   Extreme weather events don't affect only humans. Animals and animal husbandry–related industries are also impacted. Measures need to be taken to minimize the risks and deal with the outcomes.

3. In Eastern Africa, Climate Change Affects Food Security   104
   International Federation of Red Cross and Red Crescent Societies
   Droughts and floods spurred by climate change are hammering Africa's eastern nations, and they could potentially affect the area's resources.

4. Extreme Weather May Lead to Extreme Hunger   108
   Physicians for Social Responsibility
   Climate change is already affecting the planet's ability to produce enough food for its population. There is the potential for widespread famine if the trend continues.

Periodical and Internet Sources Bibliography   115

Chapter 3: Extreme Weather and Global Warming

1. Global Warming Is Man-made, Not Myth   **118**
Donald R. Prothero

Many people, including scientists, do not believe that climate change is real. But there are several thorough arguments proving that global warming is very real.

2. Is Global Warming Really That Bad?   **135**
Melissa Denchak

Yes, it really is! The concept of a warmer planet may not sound like a bad thing, but even a small change in global temperatures can have drastic effects.

3. How Much of the World Is Responsible for Global Warming?   **141**
Anup Shah

Wealthy countries have done more to contribute to global warming than developing countries, so those countries should bear a greater responsibility for emissions reductions.

4. In Southeast Asia, Cutting Greenhouse Gases Is Vital to Survival   **157**
Murray Hiebert

Following the historic Paris Climate Agreement of 2015, many countries in Southeast Asia will be watching closely to see what kinds of actions will be taken by the participating countries.

5. Whose Fault Is Climate Change?   **162**
Frank Thomas

Is climate change caused by human activity, or is it a natural cycle? There are many arguments on both sides of the issue.

Periodical and Internet Sources Bibliography   **171**

Chapter 4: Coping with Extreme Weather

1. How Various Countries Are Tackling Climate Change   **173**
NPR News Staff

Countries all over the world are being forced to deal with the consequences of global warming, while trying to plan for the future.

2. Sustainable Development Can Combat Global Disaster   181
Tom R. Burns and Nora Machado Des Johansson
Sustainability and sustainable development may hold the key to disaster risk reduction and climate change adaptation around the world.

3. Preventing Further Climate Upheaval Isn't Just the   202
Government's Domain
Bonizella Biagini and Alan Miller
It is vital that nongovernmental organizations and private businesses also engage in the efforts to cope with climate change, even though it may be difficult.

4. Europe Must Adapt to Climate Change   225
European Environment Agency
Adaptation and mitigation measures are necessary to prepare Europe for the impacts of future climate change and ensure that any extreme weather events are limited.

Periodical and Internet Sources Bibliography   232

For Further Discussion   233

Organizations to Contact   234

Bibliography of Books   238

Index   240

Foreword

*"The problems of all of humanity can
only be solved by all of humanity."*
—Swiss author Friedrich Dürrenmatt

Global interdependence has become an undeniable reality.
Mass media and technology have increased worldwide
access to information and created a society of global citizens.
Understanding and navigating this global community is a challenge,
requiring a high degree of information literacy and a new level of
learning sophistication.

Building on the success of its flagship series, Opposing
Viewpoints, Greenhaven Publishing has created the Global
Viewpoints series to examine a broad range of current, often
controversial topics of worldwide importance from a variety of
international perspectives. Providing students and other readers
with the information they need to explore global connections
and think critically about worldwide implications, each Global
Viewpoints volume offers a panoramic view of a topic of
widespread significance.

Drugs, famine, immigration—a broad, international treatment
is essential to do justice to social, environmental, health, and
political issues such as these. Junior high, high school, and early
college students, as well as general readers, can all use Global
Viewpoints anthologies to discern the complexities relating to each
issue. Readers will be able to examine unique national perspectives
while, at the same time, appreciating the interconnectedness that
global priorities bring to all nations and cultures.

Material in each volume is selected from a diverse range of
sources, including journals, magazines, newspapers, nonfiction
books, speeches, government documents, pamphlets, organization

newsletters, and position papers. Global Viewpoints is truly global, with material drawn primarily from international sources available in English and secondarily from US sources with extensive international coverage.

Features of each volume in the Global Viewpoints series include:

- An **annotated table of contents** that provides a brief summary of each essay in the volume, including the name of the country or area covered in the essay.

- An **introduction** specific to the volume topic.

- A world map to help readers locate the countries or areas covered in the essays.

- For each viewpoint, an **introduction** that contains notes about the author and source of the viewpoint explains why material from the specific country is being presented, summarizes the main points of the viewpoint, and offers three **guided reading questions** to aid in understanding and comprehension.

- **For further discussion** questions that promote critical thinking by asking the reader to compare and contrast aspects of the viewpoints or draw conclusions about perspectives and arguments.

- A worldwide list of **organizations to contact** for readers seeking additional information.

- A **periodical bibliography** for each chapter and a **bibliography of books** on the volume topic to aid in further research.

- A comprehensive **subject index** to offer access to people, places, events, and subjects cited in the text.

Global Viewpoints is designed for a broad spectrum of readers who want to learn more about current events, history, political science, government, international relations, economics, environmental science, world cultures, and sociology—students doing research for class assignments or debates, teachers and faculty seeking to supplement course materials, and others wanting to understand current issues better. By presenting how people in various countries perceive the root causes, current consequences, and proposed solutions to worldwide challenges, Global Viewpoints volumes offer readers opportunities to enhance their global awareness and their knowledge of cultures worldwide.

Introduction

> *"Changes in extreme weather threaten human health as well as prosperity. Many societies have taken measures to cope with historical weather extremes, but new, more intense extremes have the potential to overwhelm existing human systems and structures."*
> *-Climate Communication Science & Outreach*

Weather is something that humans deal with every day of their lives, no matter where they live. Some people live in mild climates with fewer extreme weather events, while others live in places where the weather is more volatile and destructive. For the most part, the varying weather events in a particular place have been a normal part of life, with a few more extreme weather events occurring at long intervals.

However, these patterns have been changing. Extreme weather, which is defined as a weather event that is significantly different from the average or usual weather pattern, is occurring more frequently. Extreme weather and climate events are classified as events that typically don't happen very often, such as floods or droughts that throughout recorded history have usually occurred only once every 100 years or so. Extreme weather also varies from normal and expected weather events in severity or duration—like a heat wave—or have a more severe impact, like hurricanes. All over the world, these types of extreme weather events are happening much more frequently than ever before, and often their destructiveness is also more intense. In its 2016 report on the status of the global climate, the United Nations World Meteorological Organization stated that 2016 would be the hottest year on record, and that global records were also set for high-impact storms, floods, wildfires, droughts, and heat waves. Because of climate change, the occurrence and impact of extreme events has risen. "'Once in a generation' heat waves and flooding are becoming more regular," the WMO's secretary-general Petteri Taalas said. "Sea level rise has increased exposure to storm surges associated with tropical cyclones."

The controversy surrounding extreme weather events has to do with the larger controversy about climate change and whether it is a real phenomenon. Scientists, politicians, and others on both sides of the issue do agree that temperatures on Earth have increased by 1.4 degrees Fahrenheit since the early twentieth century and that the levels of greenhouse gases such as carbon dioxide (CO_2) and methane (CH_4) in the atmosphere have also increased. The conflict stems from two positions. One side argues that the global temperature change and increase in greenhouse gases is due to human activities, such as the burning of fossil fuels, and that the resulting climate change is causing global warming, loss of sea ice, sea level rise, stronger storms, and more droughts. Those who believe in climate change being caused by humans also argue that it can only be slowed by international cooperation to reduce greenhouse gases. On the other side of the argument are those who feel that the amount of greenhouse gases generated by humans is too small to make a significant impact and that the Earth's atmosphere is capable of absorbing those small amounts. They contend that the global warming of the twentieth century is due to natural processes, such as fluctuation in the heat generated by the sun and the ocean's currents, and that blaming it on human action is based on misleading science and questionable measurements of temperature. As global weather patterns and events seem to change and worsen each year, there is an increasing debate between these two groups as to whether extreme weather events are simply a natural part of environmental and weather cycles, or if they are an indication that climate change is a reality and a cause for human concern.

It is nearly impossible to discuss extreme weather events without also discussing climate change. But whether one believes that Earth's climate is indeed changing—and no matter who or what is responsible for the change—extreme weather events are affecting almost everyone, no matter where they live. It is important to examine viewpoints on both extreme weather itself and its consequences, as well as if it is an indication of much bigger changes to come. These issues will be explored *in Global Viewpoints: Extreme Weather Events.*

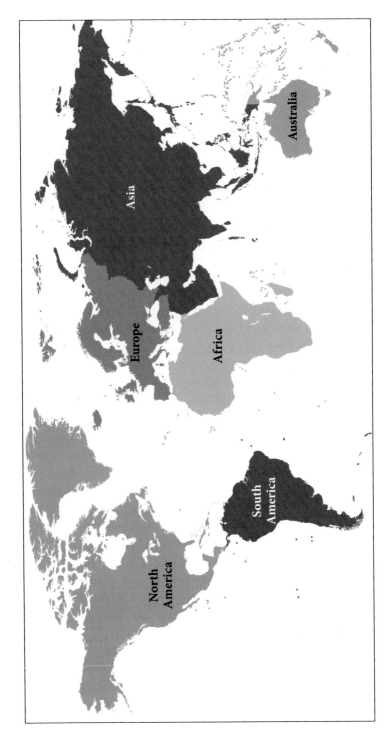

CHAPTER 1

Extreme Weather Around the World

The Global Links Between Extreme Weather and Climate Change

Daniel Huber and Jay Gulledge

In the following excerpt, Daniel Huber and Jay Gulledge argue that while climate change is usually discussed in terms of changing temperatures and precipitation, it is the increasingly extreme and severe weather events that will create the biggest social and economic costs around the world. Beyond arguing whether climate change is man-made or natural, it is more important to determine where these events are highlighting human vulnerabilities and to use that information to prioritize actions that will prevent additional damage and help humans adapt.

As you read, consider the following questions:

1. According to the authors, is climate change responsible for many more extreme weather events around the world in recent years?
2. Why is risk management an important part of looking at extreme weather trends?
3. What do recent extreme weather events indicate about larger weather trends going forward?

Thousands of record-breaking weather events worldwide bolster long-term trends of increasing heat waves, heavy precipitation, droughts and wildfires. A combination of observed trends,

"Extreme Weather and Climate Change," by Daniel Huber and Jay Gulledge, Center for Climate and Energy Solutions, December 2011. Reprinted by permission.

theoretical understanding of the climate system, and numerical modeling demonstrates that global warming is increasing the risk of these types of events today. Debates about whether single events are "caused" by climate change are illogical, but individual events offer important lessons about society's vulnerabilities to climate change. Reducing the future risk of extreme weather requires reducing greenhouse gas emissions and adapting to changes that are already unavoidable.

Introduction

Typically, climate change is described in terms of average changes in temperature or precipitation, but most of the social and economic costs associated with climate change will result from shifts in the frequency and severity of extreme events.[1] This fact is illustrated by a large number of costly weather disasters in 2010, which tied 2005 as the warmest year globally since 1880.[2] Incidentally, both years were noted for exceptionally damaging weather events, such as Hurricane Katrina in 2005 and the deadly Russian heat wave in 2010. Other remarkable events of 2010 include Pakistan's biggest flood, Canada's warmest year, and Southwest Australia's driest year. 2011 continued in similar form, with "biblical" flooding in Australia, the second hottest summer in U.S. history, devastating drought and wildfires in Texas, New Mexico and Arizona as well as historic flooding in North Dakota, the Lower Mississippi and in the Northeast.[3]

Munich Re, the world's largest reinsurance company, has compiled global disaster for 1980-2010. In its analysis, 2010 had the second-largest (after 2007) number of recorded natural disasters and the fifth-greatest economic losses.[4] Although there were far more deaths from geological disasters—almost entirely from the Haiti earthquake—more than 90 percent of all disasters and 65 percent of associated economic damages were weather and climate related (i.e. high winds, flooding, heavy snowfall, heat waves, droughts, wildfires). In all, 874 weather and climate-related disasters resulted in 68,000 deaths and $99 billion in damages worldwide in 2010.

The fact that 2010 was one of the warmest years on record as well as one of the most disastrous, begs the question: Is global warming causing more extreme weather? The short and simple answer is yes, at least for heat waves and heavy precipitation.[5] But much of the public discussion of this relationship obscures the link behind a misplaced focus on causation of individual weather events. The questions we ask of science are critical: When we ask whether climate change "caused" a particular event, we pose a fundamentally unanswerable question (see Box 1). This fallacy assures that we will often fail to draw connections between individual weather events and climate change, leading us to disregard the real risks of more extreme weather due to global warming.

Climate change is defined by changes in mean climate conditions—that is, the average of hundreds or thousands events over the span of decades. Over the past 30 years, for example, any single weather event could be omitted or added to the record without altering the long-term trend in weather extremes and the statistical relationship between that trend and the rise in global temperatures. Hence, it is illogical to debate the direct climatological link between a single event and the long-term rise in the global average surface temperature.

Nonetheless, individual weather events offer important lessons about social and economic vulnerabilities to climate change. Dismissing an individual event as happenstance because scientists did not link it individually to climate change fosters a dangerously passive attitude toward rising climate risk. The uncertainty about future weather conditions and the illogic of attributing single events to global warming need not stand in the way of action to manage the rising risks associated with extreme weather. Indeed, such uncertainty is why risk managers exist—insurance companies, for example—and risk management is the correct framework for examining the link between global climate change and extreme weather.

An effective risk management framework accommodates uncertainty, takes advantage of learning opportunities to update understanding of risk, and probes today's rare extreme events for useful information about how we should respond to rising risk. Risk management eschews futile attempts to forecast individual chaotic events and focuses on establishing long-term risk certainty; that is, an understanding of what types of risks are increasing and what can be done to minimize future damages. An understanding of the meaning of risk and how it relates to changes in the climate system is crucial to assessing vulnerability and planning for a future characterized by rising risk.

Recent Extreme Weather

Since 2010 tied with 2005 as the warmest year on record globally, it should come as no surprise that 19 countries set new national high-temperature records; this is the largest number of national high temperature records in a single year, besting 2007 by two.[6] One of the countries was Pakistan, which registered "the hottest reliably measured temperature ever recorded on the continent of Asia" (128.3 °F on May 26 in Mohenjo-daro).[7] Strikingly, no new national record low-temperatures occurred in 2010.[8] Several historic heat waves occurred across the globe, as well. Unprecedented summer heat in western Russia caused wildfires and destroyed one-third of Russia's wheat crop; the combination of extreme heat, smog, and smoke killed 56,000 people.[9] In China, extreme heat and the worst drought in 100 years struck Yunan province, causing crop failures and setting the stage for further devastation by locust swarms.[10] In the United States, the summer of 2010 featured record breaking heat on the east coast with temperatures reaching 106 degrees as far north as Maryland.[11] Records also were set for energy demand and the size of the area affected by extreme warmth.[12] Even in California where the average temperatures were below normal, Los Angeles set its all-time high temperature record of 113 degrees on September 27.

Global precipitation was also far above normal, with 2010 ranking as the wettest year since 1900.[13] Many areas received record heavy rainfall and flooding. Westward shifts of the monsoon

BOX 1: Why can't scientists say whether climate change "caused" a given weather event?

Climate is the average of many weather events over of a span of years. By definition, therefore, an isolated event lacks useful information about climate trends. Consider a hypothetical example: Prior to any change in the climate, there was one category 5 hurricane per year, but after the climate warmed for some decades, there were two category 5 hurricanes per year. In a given year, which of the two hurricanes was caused by climate change? Since the two events are indistinguishable, this question is nonsense. It is not the occurrence of either of the two events that matters. The two events together—or more accurately, the average of two events per year—define the change in the climate.

dropped 12 inches of rain across wide areas of Pakistan, flooding the Indus River valley, displacing millions of people and destabilizing an already precariously balanced nation.[14] Rio de Janeiro received the heaviest rainfall in 30 years—almost 12 inches in 24 hours, causing nearly 300 mudslides and killing at least 900 people.[15]

Developed countries also suffered debilitating downpours. On the heels of Queensland, Australia's wettest spring since 1900, December rainfall broke records in 107 locations.[16] Widespread flooding shaved an estimated $30 billion off Australia's GDP.[17] The United States experienced several record breaking torrential downpours. In Tennessee, an estimated 1,000-year flooding event[18] brought more than a foot of rain in two days, resulting in record flooding and over two billion dollars in damages in Nashville alone, equivalent to a full year of economic output for that city. In Arkansas, an unprecedented 7 inches of rain fell in a few hours, causing flash flooding as rivers swelled up to 20 feet.[19] Wisconsin had its wettest summer on record, which is remarkable given the series of historic floods that have impacted the upper Midwest over the last two decades.

In 2011, there have already been three separate historic floods in the United States, the driest 12 months ever recorded in Texas, and a record breaking tornado outbreak (see Box 2).[20] Damages from Hurricane Irene, much of which is flood related, are estimated to be between $7 and $10 billion, making it one of the top ten most damaging hurricanes ever to hit the US.[21]

The historic weather extremes of 2010 and 2011 fit into a larger narrative of damaging extreme weather events in recent decades. Recent heat waves in Russia and the United States have evoked memories of the 1995 heat wave that killed hundreds of Chicagoans, and the 2003 European heat wave that killed at least 35,000 people.[22] In the United States, the number of storms costing more than $100 million has increased dramatically since 1990. Although the 2010 flooding in the American Midwest was highly damaging, it was not on the scale of the 1993 and 2008 events, each costing billions of dollars and of such ferocity that they should be expected to occur only once in 300 years.[23] Other unprecedented disasters include the 2008 California wildfires that burned over a million acres,[24] and the decade-long Southwest drought, which continues in spite of an uncharacteristically wet winter.[25] Mumbai, India, recorded its highest ever daily rainfall with a deluge of 39 inches that flooded the city in July of 2005.[26] This neared the Indian daily record set the year before when 46 inches fell in Aminidivi, which more than doubled 30-year-old record of 22.6 inches.[27] Torrential downpours continued for the next week, killing hundreds of people and displacing as many as 1 million.[28]

Climate Trends

Taken in aggregate, this narrative of extreme events over recent decades provides a few snapshots of a larger statistical trend toward more frequent and intense extreme weather events. Rising frequency of heavy downpours is an expected consequence of a warming climate, and this trend has been observed. Some areas will see more droughts as overall rainfall decreases and other areas will experience heavy precipitation more frequently. Still other regions may not experience a change in total rainfall amounts but might see rain come in rarer, more intense bursts, potentially leading to flash

> # BOX 2: What about climate change and tornadoes?
>
> Scientists are unsure if tornadoes will become stronger or more frequent, but with increased temperatures changing the weather in unexpected ways, the risk is real that tornado outbreaks will become more damaging in the future. The lack of certainty in the state of the science does not equate with a lack of risk, since risk is based on possibility. The lack of scientific consensus is a risk factor itself, and we must prepare for a future that could possibly include increased tornado damage.

floods punctuating periods of chronic drought. Therefore, observed trends in heat, heavy precipitation, and drought in different places are consistent with global warming.[29]

Over the past 50 years, total rainfall has increased by 7 percent globally, much of which is due to increased frequency of heavy downpours. In the United States, the amount of precipitation falling in the heaviest 1 percent of rain events has increased by nearly 20 percent overall, while the frequency of light and moderate events has been steady or decreasing.[30] Meanwhile, heat waves have become more humid, thereby increasing biological heat stress, and are increasingly characterized by extremely high nighttime temperatures, which are responsible for most heat-related deaths.[31] In the western United States, drought is more frequent and more persistent, while the Midwest experiences less frequent drought but more frequent heavy precipitation.[32]

Record daytime and nighttime high temperatures have been increasing on a global scale.[33] In the United States today, a record high temperature is twice as likely to be broken as a record low, and nighttime temperature records show a strong upward trend. By contrast, record highs and lows were about equally likely in the 1950s.[34] This trend shows that the risk of heat waves is increasing over time, consistent with the results of global climate models that are forced by rising atmospheric greenhouse gas concentrations.[35] Indeed, the observed heat wave intensities in the early 21st century already exceed the worst-case projections of climate models.[36] Moreover, the distribution of observed temperatures is wider than the temperature range produced by climate models, suggesting that models may underestimate the rising risk extreme heat as warming proceeds.

Climate Change and the Rising Risk of Extreme Weather

When averaged together, changing climate extremes can be traced to rising global temperatures, increases in the amount of water vapor in the atmosphere, and changes in atmospheric circulation. Warmer temperatures directly influence heat waves and increase the moisture available in the atmosphere to supply extreme precipitation events. Expanding sub-tropical deserts swelling out from the equator are creating larger areas of sinking, dry air, thus expanding the area of land that is subject to drought.[37] The expansion of this sub-tropical circulation pattern also is increasing heat transport from the tropics to the Arctic and pushing mid-latitude storm tracks, along with their rainfall, to higher latitudes.

As discussed above, no particular short-term event can be conclusively attributed to climate change. The historical record provides plenty of examples of extreme events occurring in the distant past and such events obviously occur without requiring a change in the climate. What matters is that there is a statistical record of these events occurring with increasing frequency and/or intensity over time, that this trend is consistent with expectations from global warming, and that our understanding of climate physics indicates that this trend should continue into the future as the world continues to warm. Hence, a probability-based risk management framework is the correct way to consider the link between climate change and extreme weather.

It is also important to disentangle natural cycles from climate change, both of which are risk factors for extreme weather. Consider an analogy: An unhealthy diet, smoking, and lack of exercise are

---

BOX 3: The 2011 Texas drought: A case study in multiple risk factors

Over the past year, Texas has experienced its most intense single-year drought in recorded history. Texas State Climatologist John Nielsen-Gammon estimated the three sources of climate variability—two natural cycles plus global warming—that contributed to the drought's unprecedented intensity:

- La Nina, 79%
- Atlantic Multidecadal Oscillation, 4%
- Global Warming, 17%

Although information about uncertainty is lacking in this analysis, it clearly identifies global warming as one of the risk factors.

---

all risk factors for heart disease, and not one of these factors can or should be singled out as the cause of a particular heart attack. Similarly, a particular weather event is not directly caused by a single risk factor but has a higher probability of occurrence depending on the presence of various risk factors. The influence on risk from different sources of climate variability is additive, so global warming presents a new risk factor added on top of the natural ones that have always been with us. Over time, natural cycles will come and go, but global warming will continue in one direction such that its contribution to risk will reliably increase over time. Global warming has simply added an additional and ever rising risk factor into an already risky system (see Box 3).

Extreme events are often described by their expected frequency of recurrence. A "25-year event" has a statistical expectation of occurring once in 25 years, on average. It may occur more than once in any 25-year span or not at all for a full century, but over many centuries it is expected to occur on average once every 25 years. Events with a longer recurrence time tend to be more severe, so that a 100-year flood is a more dreaded event than a 25-year flood. A 500-year flood would be even more damaging, but it is considered to be so rare that people generally do not worry about events of such a magnitude. The problem with climate change, however, is that what used to be a 500-year event may become a 100-year or 10-year event, so that most people will experience such events within their lifetimes.

Risk cannot be thought of in a discontinuous way, with singular events having predictive power about specific future events. Risk is the accumulation of all future possibilities weighted by their probabilities of occurrence. Therefore, an increase in either disaster frequency or severity increases the risk. Events can be ordered on a future timeline and ranked by expectations about their frequency, but this only describes what we expect to happen on average over a long period of time; it does not predict individual events. Consequently, impacts are uncertain in the short term, but the risk of impacts will rise in a predictable fashion. Risk therefore tells us what future climate conditions we should plan for in order to minimize the expected costs of weather-related disasters over the lifetime of long-lived investments, such as houses, levees, pipelines, and emergency management infrastructure.

Risk management is used extensively almost anywhere decision-makers are faced with incomplete information or unpredictable outcomes that may have negative impacts. Classic examples include the military, financial services, the insurance industry, and countless actions taken by ordinary people every day. Homeowners insurance, bicycle helmets, and car seatbelts are risk-management devices that billions of people employ daily, even though most people will never need them.

Understanding Climate Risk

The extreme events cataloged above and the trends they reflect provide a proxy for the types of events society will face with greater risk in the future. With a clear record of trends and reasonable projections for the future, the level of risk can be assessed and prepared for. Risk can be thought of as a continuous range of possibilities, each with a different likelihood of occurring;

extreme outcomes reside on the low-probability tails of the range or distribution. For example, climate change is widening the probability distribution for temperature extremes and shifting the mean and the low-probability tails toward more frequent and intense heat events.

The rising risk of extreme events has much in common with playing with loaded dice, where the dice are weighted to roll high numbers more frequently. Moreover, one of the dice has numbers from two to seven instead of one to six. It is therefore possible to roll a 13 (i.e. the maximum possible temperature is higher than before) and would be more likely (because the dice are loaded) than rolling a 12 with two normal dice. The probability distribution of the loaded dice compared to normal dice is translated into changing climate risk. With normal dice, one can expect to roll snake eyes (cold extremes) about equally as often as double sixes (hot extremes). But with climate change, the dice are loaded so that cold extremes (as defined in the previous climate) are a bit less likely than they used to be and hot extremes are hotter and more likely than before.

The new risk profile presents a nonlinear increase in the number of extremes on one tail (i.e. heat waves). In light of recent cold winters in the United States and Europe, it is important to recognize that this new curve does not dispense with cold extremes, as the widening of the distribution (i.e. increase in variability) partially offsets the shift toward warmer events. Cold extremes become less frequent but do not disappear. Moreover, like heavy downpours, heavy snowfall is also consistent with global warming (see Box 4).

Under this new risk profile, the probability of record heat increases dramatically. The deadly 2003 European heat wave offers an example of a real world event that conforms to this new expectation. An event of that magnitude has a very small probability under the unchanged climate regime but has a much higher probability under a new climate profile that is both hotter and more variable. Since this event actually happened, we know that an event of that intensity is possible, and model projections tell us that the risk of such an event should be expected to rise dramatically in the coming decades due to global warming. Indeed, a 50 percent increase in variance alone, without even shifting the average temperature, could make the 2003 heat wave a 60-year event rather than a 500-year event under the old regime.[40] Other research has indicated that the risk of a 2003-type heat wave in Europe is already twice as large because of warming over recent decades. With continued warming, the frequency of such an event could rise to multiple occurrences per decade by the middle of this century.[41]

Hot extremes are not the only sort of weather event to have increased beyond expectations. Observed increases in extreme hourly precipitation are beyond projections, even while daily precipitation changes remain within expectations. This indicates that the scaling of precipitation with increases in atmospheric moisture is not consistent between short bursts and total amounts over longer periods. In the Netherlands, a study shows that one-hour precipitation extremes have increased at twice the rate with rising temperatures as expected when temperatures exceed 12°C.[43] This is another example of the type of rapid increase in extreme events that is possible when the risk distribution is not only shifted but also exhibits increased variance.

Attributing Risk and Assessing Vulnerability

It should be clear that while one cannot attribute a particular weather event to climate change, it is possible to attribute and project changes in risk of some categories of extreme weather. In order to have confidence in any climate-related risk assessment, the connection between climate change and a particular type of weather event needs to be established by multiple lines of evidence. This connection relies on three supporting avenues of evidence: theory, modeling and observation....First, scientists must understand the physical basis of why a type of weather event ought to respond to climate change. To assess whether such a response has already begun, observational data should show an increase in

BOX 4: Can global warming cause heavy snow?

In December 2009 and February 2010, several American East Coast cities experienced back-to-back record-breaking snowfalls. These events were popularly dubbed "Snowmageddon" and "Snowpocalypse." Such events are consistent with the effects of global warming, which is expected to cause more heavy precipitation because of a greater amount of water vapor in the atmosphere. Freezing temperatures are normal during the winter for cities like Washington, D.C., Philadelphia, and New York. Storms called Nor'easters are also normal occurrences. As global warming evaporates more water from the Gulf of Mexico and the Atlantic Ocean, the amount of atmospheric moisture available to fuel these storms has been increasing, thus elevating the risk of "apocalyptic" snowstorms.

frequency, duration, or intensity that is commensurate with the physical understanding. Finally, computational models forced by elevated greenhouse gas concentrations should show an increase in risk that is consistent with theory and observation.

There is supporting evidence in all three areas (theory, modeling, and observation) pointing to a global-warming induced increase in risk for four important categories of weather-related extreme events: extreme heat, heavy downpours, drought and drought-associated wildfires. For some other types of weather events, there is not sufficient evidence to conclude that global warming has increased risk. For example, evidence relating hurricane risk to climate change is "two-legged": There is a physical basis for expecting hurricanes to have stronger winds and produce more rainfall due to global warming, and models with enhanced greenhouse gas levels show an increase in the number of such storms. With two legs of the stool, hurricanes are a type of event that we should consider a potential future threat for increased risk, but more research is needed to confirm. However, observational evidence is insufficient to confirm that such a response has already begun. For tornadoes, the evidence is "zero-legged," meaning that neither theory, modeling, nor observation offer any indication of how tornado risk has changed or might change in the future due to global warming, although that does not mean there is no risk (see Box 2).

In addition to aggregate trend analysis, planners and policymakers can and do use individual extreme weather events as laboratories for assessing social and economic vulnerabilities and crafting appropriate actions to minimize the suffering and costs expected from similar events in the future. For example, in 1995 a prolonged heat wave killed hundreds in Chicago, after which the city took effective steps to prepare for future heat waves.[44] Prior to the 2003 European heat wave, the possibility that such a deadly heat wave could strike Europe had not been considered. Now that European society is aware of this possibility, preparations have been made to decrease future suffering and economic damage. Similarly, Hurricane Katrina demonstrated that a major American city can be paralyzed for weeks, without effective emergency response, communications, security, sanitation, or health care. Other recent examples of flooding and extreme rainfall should provide lessons on where flood control and emergency response systems are most needed and how much the investments in preparation are worth. Additionally, extreme events represent data points that can improve trends and estimates of future risk, as it is critically important to update trends for estimating existing risk as well as future risk.

Responding to Rising Risk

Both adapting to unavoidable climate change and mitigating future greenhouse gas emissions are required to manage the risks of extreme weather in a warmer climate. Since limiting the amount of CO_2 in the atmosphere limits the magnitude of climate change in general, reducing CO_2 emissions is effective at preventing both linear increases in risks and the more difficult to predict, nonlinear changes in extremes. Due to this property, mitigation action can be thought of as a benefit multiplier, as linear decreases in emissions can result in nonlinear decreases in extreme risk. Conversely, since climate change is already underway, some impacts are unavoidable and society must adapt to them. In order to be effective, adaptation actions must be commensurate with the magnitude of the risk. Nonlinear increases in risk associated with weather extremes require adaptation actions beyond what would be expected by looking at changes in average climate conditions. Moreover, many adaptation options are likely to be infeasible if the climate changes too much; adequate mitigation is therefore required to facilitate successful adaptation.

Science is not a crystal ball, but it offers powerful tools for evaluating the risks of climate change. Scientists can investigate whether the risk of certain types of events is rising by examining recent trends, and also whether the risks are likely to rise in the future using projections from climate models. When these two indicators converge, we should look to reduce vulnerability to such events. Indeed, a growing body of research is using climate models as a mechanism for investigating future increases in risk. Models cannot predict specific events but for some types of extremes they can indicate how risk profiles are likely to change in the future. This approach is particularly powerful when benchmarked against actual events that society agrees should be guarded against.

In 2000, the United Kingdom experienced devastating autumn floods associated with meteorological conditions that are realistically mimicked in climate models. In a climate model, the risk of severe autumn flooding increased by 20 to 90 percent under present-day greenhouse gas concentrations compared to preindustrial concentrations.[45] Conversely, modeling simulations of the deadly 2010 Russian heat wave found no evidence that climate change has so far increased the risk of such an event but did find that continued warming is very likely to produce frequent heat waves of a similar magnitude later this century.[46] Hence, regardless of the cause of that particular heat wave, the risk of similar events in the future can be expected to rise with continued warming of the global climate. Because the event was so deadly and economically harmful, the rising risk of similar events should prompt serious consideration of appropriate actions to limit and adapt to this risk. Given the uncertainties and risks, it does not make sense to focus on whether current events are supercharged by climate change. It does make sense, however, to take lessons from them about our current vulnerabilities and the risks inherent in unabated greenhouse gas emissions that drive extreme weather risks ever higher as time passes. Climate science can provide risk-based information that decision makers can use to understand how the risk is changing so that they can prioritize and value investments in prevention and adaptation.

Endnotes

1 Karl, T. R., Meehl, G. A., Miller, C. D., Hassol, S. J., Waple, A. M., & Murray, W. L. (2008). Weather and Climate Extremes in a Changing Climate; Regions of Focus: North America, Hawaii, Caribbean, and U.S. Pacific Islands. A Report by the U.S. Climate Change Science Program and the Subcommittee on Global Change Research. Washington, D.C., USA: Department of Commerce, NOAA's National Climatic Data Center.

2 National Climatic Data Center. (2010, December). State of the Climate Global Analysis: Annual 2010. Retrieved May 19, 2011, from http://1.usa.gov/fxdFai.

3 BBC News. (2011, January 1). Australia's Queensland faces "biblical" flood. Retrieved May 19, 2011, from http://bbc.in/fNzGgK; Associated Press. (2011, May 1). Federal fire crews bring expertist to huge TX fire. Retrieved May 19, 2011, from http://bit.ly/iz6JRs; Associated Press. (2011, June 16). Concern over human-caused blazes grows as wind-driven wildfires promp more evacuations. Retrieved June 22, 2011, from Washington Post: http://wapo.st/iWxirz; Sulzberger, A.G. (2011, June 26). In Minot, N.D., Flood Waters Stop Rising. Retrieved November 22, 2011, from New York Times: http://nyti .ms/ufT9jY; Doyle, R. (2011, September 8). U.S. sweltered through hottest summer in 75 years. Retrieved November 22, 2011, from USA Today: http://usat.ly/o73h4o; Robertson, C. (2011, May 15). Record Water for a Mississippi River City. Retrieved November 22, 2011, from New York Times: http://nyti.ms/lp0cTA; Freedman, A. (2011, September 12). Historic Flooding Recedes in Pennsylvania, New York; at least 15 dead. Retrieved November 22, 2011, from Washington Post: http://wapo.st/qvywOo.

4 Munich Re. (2011, February). Topics Geo Natural catastrophes 2010: Analyses, assessments, positions. Retrieved May 19, 2011, from http://bit.ly/i5zbut.

5 Karl et al., Weather and Climate Extremes in a Changing Climate, Op. cit.

6 Masters, J. (2010, August 7). Dr. Jeff Masters' WunderBlog. Retrieved May 20, 2011, from Weather Underground: http://bit.ly/dxKthO.

7 Masters, J. (2010, June 2). Dr. Jeff Masters' WunderBlog. Retrieved May 20, 2011, from Weather Underground: http://bit.ly/bDAvx2.

8 Herrera, M. (n.d.). Extreme temperatures around the world. Retrieved May 20, 2011, from http://bit.ly/crTJ2a.

9 Munich Re, Topics Geo Natural Catastrophes 2010, Op. cit.

10 National Climatic Data Center. State of the Climate Global Analysis: Annual 2010, Op.cit.

11 National Climatic Data Center. Top 10 US Weather/Climate Events of 2011. Retrieved May 19, 2011, from http://1.usa.gov/lGpdnE.

12 Ibid.

13 National Climatic Data Center (2011, January 12). 2010 Global Climate Highlights. Retrieved May 20, 2011, from http://1.usa.gov/ecwQmd.

14 National Climatic Data Center, State of the Climate Global Analysis: Annual 2010, Op.cit.

15 Biles, P. (2010, April 7). Flooding in Rio de Janeiro state kills scores. Retrieved May 19, 2011, from BBC News: http://bit.ly/kKe20D. O Globo. (2011, February 16). Número de mortos na Região Serrana já passa de 900 após chuvas de janeiro. Retrieved May 19, 2011, from O Globo: http://glo.bo/lMkp7G.

16 Australian Government Bureau of Meteorology. (2010, December 1). Queensland in spring 2010: The wettest spring. Retrieved May 19, 2011, from http://bit.ly/l0FVKs; Australian Government Bureau of Meteorology Queensland Climate Services Centre. (2010). Monthly Weather Review: Queensland December 2010. Brisbane: Commonwealth of Australia. Available at http://bit.ly/jcdZLt.

17 ABC News AU. (2011, January 18). Flood costs tipped to top $30b. Retrieved May 19, 2011, from http://bit.ly/gD7FyR.

18 US Army Corps of Engineers. (n.d.). Fact Sheet: Nashville Flood After Action Report (AAR). Retrieved May 19, 2011, from http://bit.ly/lUtgrR.

19 National Climatic Data Center, Top 10 US Weather/Climate Events of 2010, Op. cit.

20 Associated Press. (2011, November 16). Texas wildfire season roars on, with no end in sight. Retrieved November 22, 2011, from USA Today: http://usat.ly/rKqiWq.

21 Cooper, M. (2011, August 30). Hurricane Cost Seen as Ranking Among Top Ten. Retrieved November 22, 2011, from New York Times: http://nyti.ms/q0KDYG.

22 Schär, C., & Jendritzky, G. (2004). Climate change: Hot news from summer 2003. Nature , 432, 559-560.

23 Larson, L. W. (1996, June). The Great USA Flood of 1993. Retrieved May 19, 2011, from Destructive Water: Water-Caused Natural Disasters—Their Abatement and Control: http://1.usa.gov/4qyQbo; National Climatic Data Center. (2008, July 9). 2008 Midwestern U.S. Floods. Retrieved May 19, 2011, from http://1.usa.gov/iUW1MM.

24 Higgs, K. (2008, August 11). California Wildfires~FEMA EM-3287-CA Total Incidents from 6/22/08-8/11/08. Retrieved May 19, 2011, from http://1.usa.gov/knDLpr.

25 Carlton, J. (2011, March 31). Wet Winter Can't Slake West's Thirst. Retrieved May 19, 2011, from Wall Street Journal: http://on.wsj.com/gmPD3t.

26 Government of Maharashtra Department of Relief and Rehabilitation. (n.d.). Maharashtra Floods 2005. Retrieved May 19, 2011, from http://mdmu.maharashtra.gov .in/pdf/Flood/statusreport.pdf.

27 Ibid.

28 Ibid.

29 Karl et al. (2008), Op. cit.

30 Ibid.

31 Ibid; Ebi, K.L. & Meehl, G.A. (2007). The Heat is On: Climate Change & Heatwaves in the Midwest. In [Gulledge, J. & Smith, J., Eds.] Regional Impacts of Climate Change: Four Case Studies in the United States. Pew Center on Global Climate Change, Arlington, Virginia USA.

32 Karl, T. R., Melillo, J. M., & Peterson, T. C. (2009). Global Climate Change Impacts in the United States. Cambridge University Press. Available at http://1.usa.gov/7Mcd7Q.

33 Meehl, G. A., Tebaldi, C., Walton, G., Easterling, D., & McDaniel, L. (2009). The relative increase of record high maximum temperatuers compared to record low minimum temperatures in the U.S. Geophysical Research Letters , 36 (23), L23701.

34 Ibid.

35 Ebi & Meehl (2007), Op. cit.

36 Ganguly, A. R., Steinhaeuser, K., Erickson III, D. J., Branstetter, M., Parish, E. S., Singh, N., et al. (2009). Higher trends but larger uncertainty and geographic variability in 21st century temperature and heat waves. PNAS, 106 (37), 15555-15559.

40 Schar, C., Vidale, P.L., Luthi, D., Frei, C., Haberli, C., Liniger, M.A. & Appenzeller, C. (2004). The Role of Increasing Temperature Variability in European Summer Heatwaves. Nature 427, 332-336.

41 Stott, P. A., Stone, D., & Allen, M. (2004). Human contribution to the European heatwave of 2003. Nature, 432, 610-614.

43 Lenderink, G., & van Meijgaard, E. (2008). Increase in hourly precipitation extremes beyond expectations from temperature changes. Nature Geoscience, 1, 511-514.

44 Ebi & Meehl (2007), Op. cit.

45 Pall, P., Aina, T., Stone, D. A., Stott, P. A., Nozawa, T., Hilberts, A. G., et al. (2011). Anthropogenic greenhouse gas contribution to flood risk in England and Wales in autumn 2000. Nature, 470, 382-385.

46 Dole, R., Hoerling, M., Perlwitz, J., Eischeid, J., Pegion, P., Zhang, T., et al. (2011). Was there a basis for anticipating the 2010 Russian heat wave? Geophysical Research Letters, 38, L06702.

The Atlantic Ocean Brings a Wave of Climate Change

United Nations Environment Programme

This report, sponsored by the United Nations Environment Programme, explains how the oceans can influence Earth's climate, both long-term and short-term. The oceans are not only linked to the atmosphere, but together they form the most changeable part of the climate system. Ocean currents and temperatures are some of the biggest influences on climate variation.

As you read, consider the following questions:

1. What important functions do ocean currents carry out?
2. How do ocean currents affect global temperatures?
3. What negative effect could fresh meltwater from the Arctic region have on the world's oceans?

The oceans influence climate over long and short time-scales. On the longest time-scale of geologic time, the shape and location of the continents helps to determine the oceans' circulation patterns. Since continental plates drift at about 5 cm per year and mountain ranges rise by about 1 mm, it usually takes millions of years for new land formations to change the oceans. Patterns of ocean circulation and up-welling can also change much more rapidly, resulting in climate variations and fluctuations on a human time-scale. Records of global and, in particular, regional climate

"How the oceans influence climate," United Nations Environment Programme (UNEP). Reprinted by Permission.

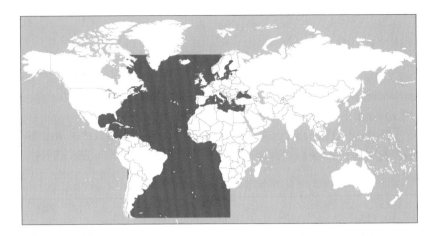

show periods lasting from years to centuries during which the climate was systematically different from earlier and later periods. Scientists believe that this behaviour is related to changes in the way the oceans store and transport heat, although the precise causes of these changes are not always clear.

The oceans and the atmosphere are tightly linked and together form the most dynamic component of the climate system. Changes in external factors such the sun's energy, the distribution of various plant species, or the emission of greenhouse gases into the atmosphere can alter the temperature and circulation patterns of the atmosphere-ocean system. Because the atmosphere and oceans are turbulent, they can also generate their own internal fluctuations. Short-term fluctuations in wind or temperature (that is, weather) can directly influence the currents and temperature of the underlying ocean, while oceanic fluctuations can magnify, diminish, or modify atmospheric fluctuations.

The oceans play a critical role in storing heat and carbon. When the earth's surface cools or is heated by the sun, the temperature change is greater—and faster—over the land than over the oceans. Because it is a fluid, the ocean diffuses the effects of a temperature change for great distances via vertical mixing and convective movements. The solid land cannot, so the sun's heat penetrates only the thin, upper crust. One consequence of the ocean's ability to absorb more heat is that when an area of ocean becomes warmer or cooler than usual, it takes much longer for that area to revert to "normal" than it would for a land area. This also explains why "maritime" climates tend to be less extreme than "continental" ones, with smaller day-night and winter-summer differences.

The ocean's waters are constantly being moved about by powerful currents. Surface currents are largely wind-driven, although the rotation of the earth, the presence of continents, and the oceans' internal dynamics also have a strong influence. Deep-ocean flow (and, to a lesser extent, surface flow) is driven by density differences produced by heating and cooling and by precipitation and evaporation (cool saline water is denser than warm fresh-water). The behaviour of the atmosphere strongly affects these density differences. For example, clouds can cool the sea by blocking the warming rays of the sun or reduce surface salinity by bringing rain. The wind can influence evaporation rates by blowing more strongly or more weakly.

These currents influence the climate by transporting heat. Horizontal currents, particularly those moving north or south, can carry warmed or cooled water as far as several thousand kilometres. The displaced water can then warm or cool the air and, indirectly, the land over which this air blows. For example, water from the tropical and subtropical Atlantic (including some from the Gulf of Mexico) moves north through the Atlantic in a current popularly (if misleadingly) called the "Gulf Stream." There it bathes the shores of Western Europe, producing a climate that is surprisingly mild for that latitude. In addition to currents, up-wellings of cold water in places where the wind blows surface water away can also affect climate. Thus San Francisco, influenced by coastal up-welling, is hardly warmer than Dublin, which is influenced by the Gulf Stream, despite being over 1,600 km further south.

Currents involved in "deep-water formation" are particularly important for climate. In winter, surface cooling causes water to become more dense. (While fresh-water that is cooled starts to expand at temperatures below 4 C, salt-water continues to compress all the way down to its freezing point of -2 C.) In areas where evaporation exceeds precipitation, the resulting rise in salinity also increases density. When the surface water becomes denser than the underlying water, "convective overturning" occurs and the dense surface water mixes downwards. In certain places this downward mixing can occasionally extend all the way to the bottom, even in deep oceans. The dense, deep water thus formed spreads out over the whole ocean. As a result, when downward mixing takes place at high latitudes it creates a circulation pattern in which warm water from tropical and subtropical regions moves pole-ward, surrenders heat to the atmosphere, cools and sinks, and flows back towards the equator. The net result is a transport of heat pole-ward.

An apparently small change in just one aspect of the ocean's behaviour can produce major climate variations over large areas of the earth. The areas of cold-water formation are one known example of this possibly widespread phenomenon. Although more research is needed, there is some agreement among oceanographers that, for the entire area north of 30 N latitude, the ocean's pole-ward transport of heat is the equivalent of about 15 watts per square metre of the earth's surface (W/m2). This can be compared with some 200 W/m2 from direct sunshine, and about 6 W/m2 for what climate change models predict will happen if the atmospheric concentration of carbon dioxide doubles. Recent observations, ocean core records, and some modeling results indicate that North Atlantic deep-water formation and its associated ocean heat flow fluctuate substantially over time-scales ranging from years to millennia. The system is vulnerable because even a relatively small decrease in surface salinity prevents water—no matter how cold it is—from sinking. This could occur if there is a flood of fresh-water run-off from the Arctic due to global warming.

Weird Weather? Blame the North Atlantic

Whether dubbed "climate extremes" or "global weirding," we have been witnessing some surprising and concerning weather events. In Europe, seasons seem to be changing, but not consistently. …In 2003, much of western Europe endured the hottest summer on record and July 2006 was the hottest month ever recorded in England—both periods were defined as heatwaves.

From 2007 onwards, the UK ran into a sequence of relatively cool, wet summers, with exceptional rainfall and widespread flooding in 2007 and 2012.

So what's behind all this extreme weather? Some have sought links to changes in the Arctic, in the tropics, or in solar activity. And all of these do influence the "jet stream" high in the atmosphere that guides and drives weather over Europe and North America.

But there's a more local factor: temperature patterns in the North Atlantic. … These changes in the Atlantic coincided with extremes across eastern North America and Europe…though other influences, such as the current El Niño, are clearly important too.

It's too early to say how much the Atlantic may have influenced strange weather elsewhere, but anomalous warmth in the western subtropics and the Gulf of Mexico late last year is also noteworthy, and may be linked to those balmy conditions in the eastern US.

Changes in weather extremes are both breathtaking in scale and serious in consequence. And it'll get worse before it gets better. Despite agreements aimed at limiting global warming to 2°C, we still face dangerous climate variability. …So as the world warms, we are carefully monitoring our oceans, and how they are interacting with the atmosphere—this is key to a better understanding of extreme weather and seasonal predictions. There has never been a more important time to get to grips with our volatile climate.

Robert Marsh and Joel Hirschi

"Weird Weather? Blame the North Atlantic," by Robert Marsh and Joel Hirschi, The Conversation, January 23, 2016. https://theconversation.com/weird-weather-blame-the-north-atlantic-53271. Licensed under CC BY-ND 4.0 International.

Climate Change and Global Warming 101

Anup Shah

In this article, GlobalIssues.org editor Anup Shah addresses some of the most common questions about climate change and global warming, greenhouse gases, and the carbon cycle, as well as how extreme weather events are related to climate change and the potential repercussions of climate change.

As you read, consider the following questions:

1. What is the greenhouse effect, and how does it affect Earth's climate?
2. How will global warming affect Earth's climate?
3. What effects will global warming have on Earth's oceans?

What Is Global Warming and Climate Change?

Global warming and climate change refer to an increase in average global temperatures. Natural events and human activities are believed to be contributing to an increase in average global temperatures. This is caused primarily by increases in greenhouse gases such as Carbon Dioxide (CO_2).

A warming planet thus leads to a change in climate which can affect weather in various ways, as discussed further below.

"Climate Change and Global Warming Introduction," by Anup Shah, Global Issues, February 1, 2015, http://www.globalissues.org/article/233/climate-change-and-global-warming-introduction. Reprinted by permission of the author.

[...]

What is the greenhouse effect?

The term *greenhouse* is used in conjunction with the phenomenon known as the *greenhouse effect*.

- Energy from the sun drives the earth's weather and climate, and heats the earth's surface;

- In turn, the earth radiates energy back into space;

- Some atmospheric gases (water vapor, carbon dioxide, and other gases) trap some of the outgoing energy, retaining heat somewhat like the glass panels of a greenhouse;

- These gases are therefore known as greenhouse gases;

- The greenhouse effect is the rise in temperature on Earth as certain gases in the atmosphere trap energy.

Six main greenhouse gases are carbon dioxide (CO_2), methane (CH_4) (which is 20 times as potent a greenhouse gas as carbon dioxide) and nitrous oxide (N_2O), plus three fluorinated industrial gases: hydrofluorocarbons (HFCs), perfluorocarbons (PFCs) and sulphur hexafluoride (SF_6). Water vapor is also considered a greenhouse gas.

The greenhouse effect is natural. What do we have to do with it?

Many of these greenhouse gases are actually life-enabling, for without them, heat would escape back into space and the Earth's average temperature would be a lot colder.

However, if the greenhouse effect becomes stronger, then more heat gets trapped than needed, and the Earth might become less habitable for humans, plants and animals.

Carbon dioxide, though not the most potent of greenhouse gases, is the most significant one. Human activity has caused an imbalance in the natural cycle of the greenhouse effect and related processes. NASA's Earth Observatory is worth quoting the effect human activity is having on the natural carbon cycle, for example:

"In addition to the natural fluxes of carbon through the Earth system, anthropogenic (human) activities, particularly fossil fuel burning and deforestation, are also releasing carbon dioxide into the atmosphere.

When we mine coal and extract oil from the Earth's crust, and then burn these fossil fuels for transportation, heating, cooking, electricity, and manufacturing, we are effectively moving carbon more rapidly into the atmosphere than is being removed naturally through the sedimentation of carbon, ultimately causing atmospheric carbon dioxide concentrations to increase.

Also, by clearing forests to support agriculture, we are transferring carbon from living biomass into the atmosphere (dry wood is about 50 percent carbon).

The result is that humans are adding ever-increasing amounts of extra carbon dioxide into the atmosphere. Because of this, atmospheric carbon dioxide concentrations are higher today than they have been over the last half-million years or longer."
— *"The Carbon Cycle; The Human Role," Earth Observatory,*
NASA

Another way of looking at this is with a simple analogy: consider salt and human health:

- A small amount of salt is essential for human life;

- Slightly more salt in our diet often makes food tastier;

- Too much salt can be harmful to our health.

In a similar way, greenhouse gases are essential for our planet; the planet may be able to deal with slightly increased levels of such gases, but too much will affect the health of the whole planet.

The other difference between the natural carbon cycle and human-induced climate change is that the latter is rapid. This means that ecosystems have less chance of adapting to the changes that will result and so the effects felt will be worse and more dramatic it things continue along the current trajectory.

[...]

Doesn't recent record cold weather disprove global warming?

In different parts of the world, there have been various weather events that at first thought would question global warming. For example, some regions have experienced extremely cold winters (sometimes record-breaking), while others have experienced heavy rain, etc.

The confusion that sometimes arises is the difference between climate change and weather patterns. Weather patterns describe short-term events, while climate change is a longer process that affects the weather. A warming planet is actually consistent with increasing cold, increasing rain and other extremes, as an overall warmer planet changes weather patterns everywhere at all times of the year.

To get an idea of how looking at short term changes only can lead to a conclusion that global warming has stopped, or doesn't exist, see Alden Griffith's online article "Has Global Warming Stopped?"

(As an aside, those crying foul of global warming claims when going through extremely cold weather in Europe for example in 2010, later found their summers to be full of heat waves. The point here is that a specific short period such as a cold winter—or even a hot summer—is not proof alone that global warming has stopped (or increased); short term variability can mask longer term trends.)

This means, for example, increasing temperatures can actually mean more snowfall—at least until it becomes too warm for significant snowfall to happen.

The additional concern, as meteorology professor Scott Mandia explains, it can take decades for the climate temperatures to increase in response to increased greenhouse gas emissions. So up until now, perhaps it has been easier for skeptics to deny climate change is occurring or that humans are responsible.

[...]

What Are the Impacts of Global Warming?

For decades, greenhouse gases, such as carbon dioxide, have been increasing in the atmosphere. But why does that matter? Won't warmer weather be nicer for everyone?

Rapid changes in global temperature

Increased greenhouse gases and the greenhouse effect has contributed to an overall warming of the Earth's climate, leading to a global warming (even though some regions may experience cooling, or wetter weather, while the temperature of the planet on average would rise).

Consider also the following:

"While year-to-year changes in temperature often reflect natural climatic variations such as El Niño/La Niña events, changes in average temperature from decade-to-decade reveal long-term trends such as global warming. Each of the last three decades has been much warmer than the decade before. At the time, the 1980s was the hottest decade on record. In the 1990s, every year was warmer than the average of the previous decade. The 2000s were warmer still."

—*"Past Decade Warmest on Record According to Scientists in 48 Countries, National Ocean and Atmospheric Administration (NOAA),"* July 28, 2010

At the end of the 1990s, the World Meteorological Organization (WMO) had noted that not only was the 1990s the warmest decade but at the time, the 1900s was the warmest century during the last 1,000 years.

It is the rapid pace at which the temperature will rise that will result in many negative impacts to humans and the environment and this why there is such a world-wide concern.

Small average global temperature change can have a big impact

Climate scientists admit that the chances of the world keeping average global temperature at current levels are not going to be possible (humanity has done little to address things in the past couple of decades that these concerns have been known about).

So, now, there is a push to contain temperature rises to an average 2°C increase (as an average, this means some regions may get higher temperatures and others, lower).

Even just a 2°C increase can have impacts around the world to biodiversity, agriculture, the oceans etc (detailed further below). But in the lead up to important global climate talks at the end of 2009, some delegates are skeptical that temperature rises can be contained to a 2°C rise (or CO_2 levels of 350 ppm).

[...]

Extreme weather patterns

Most scientists believe that the warming of the climate will lead to more extreme weather patterns such as:

- More hurricanes and drought;

- Longer spells of dry heat or intense rain (depending on where you are in the world);

- Scientists have pointed out that Northern Europe could be severely affected with colder weather if climate change continues, as the arctic begins to melt and send fresher waters further south. It would effectively cut off the Gulf Stream that brings warmth from the Gulf of Mexico, keeping countries such as Britain warmer than expected;

- In South Asia, the Himalayan glaciers could retreat causing water scarcity in the long run.

While many environmental groups have been warning about extreme weather conditions for a few years, the World Meteorological Organization announced in July 2003 that "Recent scientific assessments indicate that, as the global temperatures continue to warm due to climate change, the number and intensity of extreme events might increase."

The WMO also notes that "New record extreme events occur every year somewhere in the globe, but in recent years the number of such extremes have been increasing." (The WMO limits the definition of extreme events to high temperatures, low temperatures and high rainfall amounts and droughts.) The U.K's *Independent* newspaper described the WMO's announcement as unprecedented and astonishing because it came from a respected United Nations organization not an environmental group!

Super-storms

Mentioned further above was the concern that more hurricanes could result. The link used was from the environmental organization WWF, written back in 1999. In August/September 2004 a wave of severe hurricanes left many Caribbean islands and parts of South Eastern United States devastated. In the Caribbean many lives were lost and there was immense damage to entire cities. In the U.S. many lives were lost as well, some of the most expensive damage resulted from the successive hurricanes.

In its wake, scientists have reiterated that such super-storms may be a sign of things to come. Global warming may spawn more super-storms, Inter Press Service (IPS) notes.

Interviewing a biological oceanography professor at Harvard University, IPS notes that the world's oceans are approaching 27 degrees C or warmer during the summer. This increases the odds of major storms.

- When water reaches such temperatures, more of it evaporates, priming hurricane or cyclone formation.

- Once born, a hurricane needs only warm water to build and maintain its strength and intensity.

Furthermore, as emissions of greenhouse gases continue to trap more and more of the sun's energy, that energy has to be dissipated, resulting in stronger storms, more intense precipitation and higher winds.

"There is abundant evidence of an unprecedented number of severe weather events in the past decade, [professor of biological oceanography at Harvard University, James] McCarthy says. In 1998, Hurricane Mitch killed nearly 20,000 people in Central America, and more than 4,000 people died during disastrous flooding in China. Bangladesh suffered some of its worst floods ever the following year, as did Venezuela. Europe was hit with record floods in 2002, and then a record heat wave in 2003.

More recently, Brazil was struck by the first-ever recorded hurricane in the South Atlantic last March.

Weather records are being set all the time now. We're in an era of unprecedented extreme weather events, McCarthy said.

Historical weather patterns are becoming less useful for predicting the future conditions because global warming is changing ocean and atmospheric conditions.

In 30 to 50 years' time, the Earth's weather generating system will be entirely different, he predicted."

— *Stephen Leahy, "Global Warming May Spawn More Super-Storms," Inter Press Service, September 20, 2004*

Extreme weather events on the increase

Looking at 2010 as a whole year revealed a variety of extreme weather events. A panel of climate and weather experts ranked the top 10 global weather/climate events of 2010 which included heat waves to droughts to negative arctic oscillation (a climate pattern where cold Arctic air slides south while warmer air moves north, bringing snow storms and record cold temperatures to much of the Northern Hemisphere) show that a variety of weather events can occur as a result of changing climate:

- **Russo-European-Asian Heat Waves.** (Summer) A severe summer spawned drought, wildfires and crop failures across western Russia, where more than 15,000 people died. All-time high temperatures occurred in many cities and nations in the region. China faced locust swarms during July.

- **2010 as [near] warmest on record.** (Calendar Year) According to NOAA, the globally-averaged temperature for 2010 will finish among the two warmest, and likely the warmest, on record. Three months in 2010 were the warmest on record for that month.

- **Pakistani Flooding.** (Late July into August) Rainfall related to the Asian Monsoon was displaced unusually westward, and more than a foot of rain fell across a large area of the Upper Indus Valley. Subsequent flooding down the Indus River killed 1,600 people and displaced millions.

- **El Niño to La Niña Transition.** (Mid-to-Late Boreal Spring) ENSO, the most prominent and far-reaching patterns of climate variability, saw a huge swing in mid-2010. Only 1973, 1983 and 1998 have seen larger within-year swings.

- **Negative Arctic Oscillation.** (December–February) The AO Index, which is strongly correlated with wintertime cold air outbreaks, reached -4.27 for February, the largest negative anomaly since records began in 1950. Major cold air outbreaks occurred throughout the Northern Hemisphere.

- **Brazilian Drought.** (Ongoing) A severe drought parching northern Brazil shrunk the Rio Negro, one of the Amazon River's most important tributaries, to its lowest level since records began in 1902 at its confluence with the Amazon. The Amazon's depth there fell more than 12 feet below its average.

- **Historically Inactive NE Pacific Hurricane Season.** (May 15‑November 30) The Northeast Pacific Hurricane Season was one of the least active on record, produced the fewest named storms and hurricanes of the modern era, and had the earliest cessation of tropical activity (Sep 23) on record.

- **Historic N. Hemispheric Snow Retreat.** (January through June) Despite December 2009 having the second-largest snow cover extent of the satellite record (mid-1960s), the melt season was ferocious, contributing to spring floods in the Northern U.S. and Canada. Following the early and pronounced snow melt, the North American, Eurasian and Hemispheric snow cover was the smallest on record for May and June 2010.

- **Minimum Sea Ice Extent.** (Mid-September) The 2010 sea ice minimum of 4.9 million sq km was the third smallest on record. The last four years (2007-2010) are the four smallest on record. The Northwest Passage and the Northern Sea Route were simultaneously ice-free in September, a first in modern history.

- **China Drought.** (First half of 2010) A persistent drought centered in the Yunan Province was touted as perhaps the worst in this region in more than 100 years. Major crop losses and lack of drinking water created severe problems for local residents.

— *Source: Top Ten Global Weather/Climate Events of 2010, National Climatic Data Center, NOAA, December 2010*

Ecosystem impacts

With global warming on the increase and species' habitats on the decrease, the chances for various ecosystems to adapt naturally are diminishing.

Many studies have pointed out that the rates of extinction of animal and plant species, and the temperature changes around the world since the industrial revolution, have been significantly different to normal expectations.

An analysis of population trends, climate change, increasing pollution and emerging diseases found that 40 percent of deaths in the world could be attributed to environmental factors.

Jaan Suurkula, M.D. and chairman of Physicians and Scientists for Responsible Application of Science and Technology (PSRAST), paints a dire picture, but notes that he is only citing observations and conclusions from established experts and institutions. Those observations and conclusions note that global warming will lead to the following situations, amongst others:

- Rapid global heating according to a US National Academy of Science warning;
- Dramatic increase in greenhouse gas emissions;
- Ozone loss aggravated by global warming;
- Ozone loss likely to aggravate global warming;
- Warming of the oceans leads to increased greenhouse gasses;
- Permafrost thawing will aggravate global warming;
- Oceanic changes observed that may aggravate the situation;
- A vicious circle whereby each problem will exacerbate other problems which will feedback into each other;
- Massive extinction of species will aggravate the environmental crisis;
- Sudden collapse of biological and ecological systems may occur, but will have a very slow recovery;
- While effective measures can decrease global warming and other problems the World community has repeatedly failed to establish cooperation.

The vicious circle Suurkula refers to is worth expanding. In his own words, but slightly reformatted:

"The ongoing accumulation of greenhouse gasses causes increasing global warming.

This causes a more extensive destruction of ozone in the polar regions because of accentuated stratospheric cooling.

An increase of ozone destruction increases the UV-radiation that, combined with higher ocean temperature, causes a reduction of the gigantic carbon dioxide trapping mechanism of the oceanic phytoplankton biomass;

This accentuates the warming process.

When the warming has reached a certain level, it will release huge amounts of greenhouse gasses trapped in the permafrost.

This will enhance the global warming, and the polar destruction of ozone, and so on.

The observed decrease of the thermohaline circulation [the various streams that transport warm and cold waters around the world and therefore has an important stabilizing effect on world climate] further aggravates the situation.

This is a global self-reinforcing vicious circle accelerating the global warming."

— Jaan Suurkula, "World-wide cooperation required to prevent global crisis; Part one—the problem," Physicians and Scientists for Responsible Application of Science and Technology, February 6, 2004

Rising sea levels

Water expands when heated, and sea levels are expected to rise due to climate change. Rising sea levels will also result as the polar caps begin to melt.

Rising sea levels are already affecting many small islands.

The WorldWatch Institute reports that "[t]he Earth's ice cover is melting in more places and at higher rates than at any time since record keeping began. (March 6, 2000)."

Rising sea levels will impact many coastlines, and a large mass of humanity lives near the coasts or by major rivers. Analysis by the World Wildlife Fund has found that many cities are unprepared for climate change effects such as rising sea levels.

Increasing ocean acidification

Although it has gained less mainstream media attention, the effects of increasing greenhouse emissions—in particular carbon dioxide—on the oceans may well be significant.

These are the 3 main concepts:

1. More CO_2 in the atmosphere means more CO_2 in the ocean;

2. Atmospheric CO_2 is dissolved in the ocean, which becomes more acidic; and

3. The resulting changes in the chemistry of the oceans disrupts the ability of plants and animals in the sea to make shells and skeletons of calcium carbonate, while dissolving shells already formed.

Scientists have found that oceans are able to absorb some of the excess CO_2 released by human activity. This has helped keep the planet cooler than it otherwise could have been had these gases remained in the atmosphere.

However, the additional excess CO_2 being absorbed is also resulting in the acidification of the oceans: When CO_2 reacts with water it produces a weak acid called carbonic acid, changing the sea water chemistry. As the Global Biodiversity Outlook report explains, the water is some 30% more acidic than pre-industrial times, depleting carbonate ions—the building blocks for many marine organisms.

In addition, concentrations of carbonate ions are now lower than at any time during the last 800,000 years. The impacts on ocean biological diversity and ecosystem functioning will likely be severe, though the precise timing and distribution of these impacts are uncertain.

Although millions of years ago CO_2 levels were higher, today's change is occurring rapidly, giving many marine organisms too little time to adapt. Some marine creatures are growing thinner shells or skeletons, for example. Some of these creatures play a crucial role in the food chain, and in ecosystem biodiversity.

Some species may benefit from the extra carbon dioxide, and a few years ago scientists and organizations, such as the European Project on Ocean Acidification, formed to try to understand and assess the impacts further.

One example of recent findings is a tiny sand grain-sized plankton responsible for the sequestration of 25–50% of the carbon the oceans absorb is affected by increasing ocean acidification. This tiny plankton plays a major role in keeping atmospheric carbon dioxide (CO_2) concentrations at much lower levels than they would be otherwise so large effects on them could be quite serious.

Other related problems reported by the Inter Press Service include more oceanic dead zones (areas where there is too little oxygen in the sea to support life) and the decline of important coastal plants and forests, such as mangrove forests that play an important role in carbon absorption. This is on top of the already declining ocean biodiversity that has been happening for a few decades, now.

Scientists now believe that ocean acidification is unparalleled in the last 300 million years, raising the possibility that we are entering an unknown territory of marine ecosystem change.

Increase in pests and disease
An increase in pests and disease is also feared.

A report in the journal *Science* in June 2002 described the alarming increase in the outbreaks and epidemics of diseases throughout the land and ocean based wildlife due to climate changes.

One of the authors points out that, "Climate change is disrupting natural ecosystems in a way that is making life better for infectious diseases."

Failing agricultural output; increase in world hunger
The *Guardian* summarizes a United Nations warning that, "One in six countries in the world face food shortages this year because of severe droughts that could become semi-permanent under climate change."

Drought and desertification are starting to spread and intensify in some parts of the world already.

Agriculture and livelihoods are already being affected
Failing agriculture in the future have long been predicted.

Looking to 2100, scientists who looked at projections of global warming's impact on the average temperatures during the growing season fear that rising temperatures will have a significant impact upon crop yields, most noticeably in the tropics and sub tropics.

While warm weather can often be good for some crops, hotter than average temperatures for the entire season is often not good for plants.

This would affect at least half the world's population that either live in the region or rely on food coming from that region.

IRIN (Integrated Regional Information Networks), part of the United Nations, has produced a series of short videos showing how some regions are already being affected by climate change and are trying to adapt as a result.

One example is farmers in Nepal finding that cultivating rice isn't as productive as before, and are changing to other crops as a result.

In some cases, improved agricultural techniques may help, such as rainwater harvesting and drip irrigation. Some also believe genetically modified crops may be essential to deal with changing climates. Yet, there are many other crucial issues that affect agriculture, such as poverty, political and economic causes of world hunger, global trade policies (which create unequal trade and affect the poorest countries the most), etc.

Women face brunt of climate change impacts

It is recognized that poorer nations will suffer the worst from climate change, either because of geographical reasons, and/or because they will have less resources to cope with a problem (mostly caused by emissions from rich countries over the past decades).

In addition to poor countries, women are likely to suffer the worst, as the United Nations Population fund explains:

> "Women—particularly those in poor countries—will be affected differently than men. They are among the most vulnerable to climate change, partly because in many countries they make up the larger share of the agricultural work force and partly because they tend to have access to fewer income-earning opportunities. Women manage households and care for family members, which often limits their mobility and increases their vulnerability to

sudden weather-related natural disasters. Drought and erratic rainfall force women to work harder to secure food, water and energy for their homes. Girls drop out of school to help their mothers with these tasks. This cycle of deprivation, poverty and inequality undermines the social capital needed to deal effectively with climate change."

— *"Facing a changing world: women, population and climate,"*
State of the World's Population 2009, UNFPA, November 18,
2009.

Coastal Resilience Is Key for the US and the World

Erin A. Thead

One of the recent indicators of a change in Earth's climate, and one that will continue to worsen, is the rise in sea levels. In the following viewpoint, atmospheric scientist and climate/resilience writer Erin Thead discusses the potential impact of sea level rise on cities around the world and the plans that many of these cities are making to help deal with rising water levels.

As you read, consider the following questions:

1. What factors affect the rate and impact of sea level change in different parts of the globe?
2. What is an example of a US city that is starting to plan for sea level rise?
3. What are some of the strategies that coastal cities will be considering when it comes to resilience planning?

A Growing Concern

Recently, a team of scientists published a study that found that the rate of sea level rise in the 20th century was greater than it had been in 2,800 years. Sea levels have risen almost 3 inches globally in the most recent 20 years and rise on an average of 1/8 inch each year. Melting land ice is responsible for a larger—and ever-increasing—amount of the global sea level rise in recent decades,

"Sea Level Rise: Risk and Resilience in Coastal Cities," by Erin A. Thead, Climate Institute, October 2016. Reprinted by permission.

as opposed to thermal expansion of seawater. A compounding problem with ice melt is that it can accelerate through positive feedback. Snow-covered ice has a high reflectivity or albedo, which means that radiation is reflected back from it and not as much is absorbed as heat. Water, however, has a very low albedo and does absorb high amounts of solar radiation and heat held in the earth's lower atmosphere. Once ice has started melting, the process accelerates without an external influence to cause refreezing. Short-term climatic patterns that temporarily raise global temperature averages, such as a strong El Niño event, can therefore exacerbate the long-term trend unless a strong cooling event occurs quickly thereafter.

The current best estimates predict that sea level will rise up to 6.6 feet, or 2 meters, by the year 2100. Until recent years, this figure was viewed as pessimistic, with a rise of 3 feet considered more likely. Recent studies raise the concern that the 6.6-foot estimate is actually the more probable one with "business as usual" carbon emissions. Earlier work accounted for glacial and Arctic melt, but had greater uncertainty about the West Antarctic Ice Sheet. The new research, developed in the last three years, modeled that the West Antarctic sheet would be undermined by warmed seawater, accelerating its decline. The study also found that adhering to the agreements in the Paris climate summit of 2015, and thereby keeping the mean global temperature increase under 2°C, would lessen the melting of the West Antarctic Ice Sheet. Nonetheless, even in this optimistic case, some sea level rise will continue to occur due to current greenhouse gas levels in the atmosphere and the attendant warming.

Coastal Resilience in the United States

Several American coastal cities have begun plans to minimize the effects of sea level rise. In New York City, the areas of the city that are in the "100-year flood zone" and "500-year flood zone"—in other words, that have a 1 percent chance and 0.2 percent chance of flooding each year—are expected to expand....

In response to the flood analysis and the destruction wrought by Sandy, the city developed a comprehensive resilience plan. In this plan, the city specifically analyzed the effects of Sandy as a near-worst-case impact and the projected future flood zones. It determined several actions to take to minimize the risks. To protect coasts against tidal flooding, the city plans to reinforce beaches, build bulkheads, and protect sand dunes that act as natural barriers. The city may also enact rock breakwaters offshore to attenuate waves associated with storms, and erect storm walls and levees in areas that are particularly vulnerable to storm surge. The city's plan contains a rigorous geological analysis of the landscape and makes recommendations specific to boroughs and neighborhoods based on what types of mitigation strategies the rock and soil in each locale can support.

Boston is another American city that has developed a comprehensive climate resiliency plan. Since it is on a coastline, Boston's greatest risks from climate change are flooding and storm surge. Boston's plan emphasizes community awareness and education as critical tools for climate preparedness. As Brian Swett, a lead developer of Boston's climate plan and formerly the chief of Boston's Department of Environment, stated with regard to storm surge,

"If I told somebody, even in July, that we're expecting 20 inches of snow in two days, everybody has that mental checklist up here in Boston: Make sure I know where the shovel is; I know the streets not to park on because there'll probably be a parking ban; I got my bread and my milk; I've got salt for the walkway. We don't have that mental checklist up here for hurricanes and we certainly don't drill for it."

The Boston climate plan also puts emphasis on outreach to low-income households, small business owners, and other vulnerable residents, by working closely with other city departments that focus on these residents' concerns. Low-income residents in particular utilize public services such as buses more than other residents, and as the tragedy of Hurricane Katrina in New Orleans showed, these residents are most vulnerable in the event of a needed evacuation.

Cities that have smaller populations than the East Coast metropolises and rely heavily on tourism for economic development are also making preparations. Tybee Island, a barrier island near Savannah, Georgia, is a popular tourist destination during the summer months. The sea level on this island's coastline has risen 10-11 inches since 1935, and as in most areas of the world, it is expected to continue rising. The city, also named Tybee Island, developed a resilience plan to cope with rising sea levels. The city has a single road that allows access on and off the island, so shoring up this road—U.S. Highway 80—and improving it to minimize traffic bottlenecks was a key part of the city's resilience plan. As in other cities, reinforcing natural barriers to inland flooding was also important, so protecting Tybee Island's beaches from erosion was another crucial part of the plan.

Coastal Resilience Around the Globe

Cities elsewhere around the world have begun to grapple with the risks of sea level rise as well. In Australia, coastal cities face the threats of tidal flooding, non-tropical storm flooding, and tropical cyclone storm surge just as cities in the U.S. do.

Australian states and municipalities also have significant authority over their own policies, comparably to the U.S. The national government of Australia has issued a strategic plan for climate resilience and adaption, which recommends procedures to states and municipalities.

The Australian resilience plan acknowledged that coastal cities were built with the assumption that weather and tidal conditions would fall within a known historical range that includes a stable sea level, and therefore that expected rises from climate change pose a threat. The government of Australia is in the process of developing an online tool, known as CoastAdapt, that will help local officials understand specific risks their areas face and provide specialized information about resilience options.

A specific example of this type of local resilience planning is the analysis of seawalls in Sydney. The city has several older seawalls, and authorities were unsure of their reliability in the face of climate change and extreme events. The government of Australia oversaw a project to assess the seawalls for their current condition that included analysis of the materials used in the seawalls, maintenance, stability, and strength. The project officials then proposed improvement suggestions for each seawall examined.

Many cities in Europe are also vulnerable to sea level rise. European cities are not at risk of hurricane storm surge due to their northerly latitudes and location on coastlines that do not experience tropical cyclones, but they are vulnerable to tidal flooding and non-tropical storm flooding. Some are also built below sea level and rely on levees for protection.

An example of the latter is the city of Rotterdam in the Netherlands, which is 90 percent below sea level and surrounded by several rivers. Dikes protect the city from inundation. In 1953, Rotterdam suffered an extremely deadly flood that breached the dikes, killing 1,800 people, a tragedy that foreshadowed Hurricane Katrina in New Orleans fifty-two years later. In response, the Dutch government directed funding to a massive project to build dikes around areas of the city. Unfortunately, over the years the structures have damaged the environment and aquatic ecosystems. In a more sustainable, ecologically sound, and physically robust plan, the government is now shoring up the natural coastline of the city by rebuilding sand dunes and expanding shores with sediment.

Lessons and Strategies for Resilience

As we have seen, governments at all levels are assessing the dangers for specific locations and analyzing the current infrastructure the world over. It is possible to model expected flood risk at an extremely high resolution and perform engineering analyses on existing infrastructure—natural and manmade—with a great degree of precision. The results are a set of plans tailored for the specific needs and capabilities of each location. Climate change does not affect all parts of the earth in the same way, and even sea level rise will not be globally uniform, so highly individualized resilience planning is a must. Their diversity notwithstanding, however, the plans do have some things in common. The ideas that appear repeatedly, in resilience plans around the globe, do so because they are broadly applicable, and in many cases, planners have arrived at them through past experience. Cities that wish to develop their own coastal resilience plans should look to these repeat ideas as guidance.

First, coastal cities at particular risk of flooding should protect any natural barrier islands that are present. These islands are the first line of defense against storm surge, whether from tropical cyclones or other storms at sea. Cities that can afford it, and can do so in an environmentally friendly way, might follow the example of New York City and erect artificial breakwaters offshore if they do not have any natural barrier islands. These structures could also serve as artificial reefs for marine life if oceanic conditions permit.

Many coastal cities have artificial seawalls and levee structures. These structures tend not to be as robust against extreme events as natural barriers, but cities that have them should follow the example of Sydney and examine them in close detail to determine their robustness. Of course, to be fully effective, civil authorities should conduct this type of analysis with an eye to the specific level and type of risk that a given city is expected to face from sea level rise. Resilience planners in very low-lying locations should also keep in mind the lessons of New Orleans and Rotterdam, emphasizing shoreline and wetland restoration as the first and best defense instead of relying wholly on a system of levees to fight the natural course of rivers. For locations that are below sea level, natural restoration approaches are more robust against flooding and have proved far better for surrounding ecosystems. Cities should not neglect existing seawalls and levee structures, but they should be part of a broader strategy.

Finally, resilience analysts should always consider the human factor, particularly in the context of extreme flood events that would pose a high threat to life and require partial or full evacuation of the city during the emergency. This type of risk is especially acute for cities that are low-lying, prone to storms, or located at the mouths of significant river systems. Officials should take guidance from Boston's plan, which emphasizes promoting community education about the flood threat and devoting special attention to vulnerable populations that rely on public services. The plan for Tybee Island, a much smaller municipality, takes into account its reliance on tourism and the dependence of its evacuation route on a single highway. Planners should always consider the specific local needs of a city, whatever its size.

Climate change is already causing sea levels worldwide to rise, and we can only expect this trend to continue. Our best, most current science predicts that ice cap melting and thermal expansion of seawater will produce a combined average rise of up to 6.6 feet by the beginning of the next century. This level of rise would inundate some beaches and overflow many barrier islands that serve as natural protection against storm surge from tropical and non-tropical cyclones. It would also raise the risk of tidal flooding, and in areas that are expected to see an increase in rainfall, flash flooding and river flooding would compound the flood risk associated with coastal waters. The risks of sea level rise to coastal cities must be taken seriously, and the kinds of concrete, specific, individually tailored flood resilience plans illustrated here are a very positive step. While emissions reductions can lessen the magnitude of this impact, some rise is going to occur. It is imperative for areas at risk to adapt to this new hazard, and fortunately, they are beginning to do just that. These pioneering coastal cities have created plans that offer excellent guidance. Hopefully, resilience planners in other locations around the world will follow their lead.

In the US, Hurricanes Are a Harbinger of Climate Doom

John McQuaid

In the following viewpoint, science and environment journalist John McQuaid discusses the increasing severity of hurricanes and how it is related to changing global temperatures. He presents both sides of the argument that hurricanes may be increasing in frequency and severity because of global warming, and addresses the importance of observation and modeling to help predict when more dangerous storms are going to occur.

As you read, consider the following questions:

1. Do scientists agree on the relationship between hurricanes and global warming?
2. What is the link between oceans, climate, and hurricanes?
3. Does McQuaid feel that more frequent and severe hurricanes are a trend, or just a cycle?

When it engulfed swaths of coastal New York and New Jersey, Hurricane Sandy became an instant symbol of a new age of extreme weather fueled by climate change. New York Mayor Michael Bloomberg endorsed President Obama to nudge him to address climate. *Bloomberg Businessweek* summed up this sentiment with its Sandy cover story, "It's Global Warming, Stupid." But is it, really? As one of the most extreme kinds of extreme weather,

"Hurricanes and Climate Change," by John McQuaid, WGBH Educational Foundation. Reprinted by permission.

hurricanes already pose a mortal threat to anyone living along the Atlantic and Gulf Coasts and other tropical cyclone trouble spots. If we face the prospect of routine superstorms amped up by the extra heat and moisture from global warming—or, in the case of Sandy, merging with other systems into freakish weather hybrids—that's a truly apocalyptic threat.

But like many questions in science, this isn't a case of straightforward cause and effect. Many scientists accept the broad premise that a hotter climate likely contributes to some increase in hurricane strength, that this process is already underway, and that it will intensify. There's also unambiguous evidence that sea level rise, another product of climate change, will contribute to higher, more dangerous hurricane storm surges.

Beyond that, though, the science gets more speculative, as it's based on computer models tracking the complex dynamics of climate and weather and an at-times spotty record of hurricane data. There's a lot of uncertainty built in. Here's a look at what we know, and don't know, about global warming and hurricanes.

Hurricanes are, in effect, giant heat engines. They transfer latent heat energy from the ocean to the atmosphere, transforming some of it into mechanical energy in the process: the maelstrom of hurricane-force winds and giant waves. If you pump more heat into such a system, warming up the atmosphere and the ocean, it stands to reason that the venting will grow stronger. "High sea surface temperatures lead to the evaporation of moisture, which provides fuel for the storm. Then it gives up the latent heat: that is what powers the storm. Together they provide for stronger storms. The evidence is abundantly clear," says Kevin Trenberth, a senior scientist at the NOAA's National Center for Atmospheric Research in Boulder, Colorado.

Trenberth's advice? Just look at Sandy. Sea surface temperatures off the East Coast were about 3 degrees Celsius above average at the time Sandy approached. Perhaps 0.6 degrees of that, Trenberth says, is attributable to global warming. With each degree rise in sea surface temperature, the atmosphere holds 4% more moisture, which may have boosted rainfall by as much as 5% to 10% over what it would have been 40 years ago.

A Vexing Question

Scientists have wrestled with this question for decades, trying to understand the systematic relationships between climate, oceans, and hurricanes. MIT climatologist Kerry Emanuel first suggested a link between climate and hurricanes in a 1987 paper, which proposed a new method for measuring overall hurricane force. Normal measurements such as barometric pressure, maximum strength (based on wind speed), or size, are constantly changing, and thus don't tell you much about the storm's overall performance. Instead, he came up with an absolute baseline called the "power dissipation," roughly equivalent to the total amount of energy a storm expends over its lifetime, which can last weeks. (In physics, "power" is a measurement of energy expended over time.)

Global temperatures have risen about 0.5 degrees C since the 1970s, sea surface temperatures in hurricane zones by about the same amount. Emanuel's analysis of past storm data shows this has fueled the cumulative violence of cyclones, far beyond what his initial theories predicted. The overall power dissipation of Atlantic storms rose by about 60%, according to a 2007 paper. The potential intensity, a measure of the upper limit of a storm's strength, had gone up by 10%. Both the average duration and the top speed of storms had also increased, the latter by 25%.

Some, but not all, of this extra heat is the result of growing amounts of carbon dioxide and other greenhouse gases, Emanuel says. Some is due to natural causes such as volcanic eruptions. And ironically, better environmental regulations also seem to be contributing to the problem. The Clean Air Act limited the emissions of sulfate aerosols, microscopic particles produced in the burning of fossil fuels. But these particulates had a hidden, beneficial effect: the haze they create reflects some sunlight back into space. Without them, the atmosphere traps more heat.

If Emanuel is correct, then can we see the footprint of global warming when a huge storm hits? Not necessarily. Landfalling storms may be the only ones that matter to most people, but they are only a fraction of the total, a transient snapshot.

"When we look at storms over their whole lifetimes, that's a whole lot more information than you get with high intensity storms at the point they are affecting land," Emanuel says. Hurricanes that hit land make up a small dataset with a lot of statistical noise, in which warmer temperatures are just one factor. So far, it doesn't show any climate signals. "One thing that makes it very complicated from the viewpoint of climate scientists: in the case of global mean temperatures, we have records going back to the 1800s showing warming as a significant trend. But if you look back at landfalling hurricanes, there's no trend we can identify," says Tom Knutson, a research meteorologist at NOAA's Geophysical Fluid Dynamics Lab in Princeton, N.J. It will take decades, Emanuel says, before scientists have enough data to establish the connection between climate and landfalling storms.

Evidence of a Trend, or Just a Cycle?

Emanuel has his detractors, including Christopher Landsea, a meteorologist at the National Hurricane Center, who say that he and other modelers overestimate the likely boost in hurricane effects, in part because their data is incomplete. In papers and public talks, Landsea has suggested the global warming effect on hurricanes is virtually insignificant—an increase of about 1 to 2 mph in top windspeed, he says. Landsea believes that the flux in hurricane frequency and strength, including the past decade's more active hurricane trend, can be better explained by cyclic ups and downs called the Atlantic Multidecadal Oscillation. Emanuel doubts the AMO's existence: he believes it's the result of reading too much into ambiguous data. Their debate is as old as climate science itself, having roots in an ongoing split in perspective between climate modelers and meteorologists.

If coastal cities are still there in 2100, what kind of hurricane threats will they face? Climate modelers trying to answer those questions have wrestled for years with a difficult problem—climate models operate on a global scale, while the weather models used to predict hurricane strength and tracks are much more fine-grained. Putting them together to predict how climate will affect storms decades in the future risks compounding uncertainties in both models.

One of the biggest of those? The current understanding of hurricanes, as well as most of the hard data scientists input into their models, comes from satellite observation. But reliable weather satellite data goes back only about 40 years, a short time span on which to base your prediction of future trends. Yet as computing power has grown, the models have improved.

Last year, Knutson and other modelers at the NOAA Geophysical Fluid Dynamics Lab took established climate models and embedded an established hurricane forecasting model within them. This way they could successfully model past hurricane seasons and then extend those trends ahead to 2100, as sea levels rose and the atmosphere grew hotter. Different climate models spit out different pictures of the future, so they ended up with an assortment of scenarios. But a couple of trends were clear. Overall, the number of tropical cyclones fell, while the frequency of strong storms—Category 4 and 5 on the Saffir-Simpson scale—nearly doubled.

There are a couple of reasons for this mixed result. Hurricane formation depends on a low level of windshear in the upper atmosphere—that is, the difference in windspeeds at adjacent levels. Pronounced windshear lops off the top of a forming storm and makes it dissipate. Warmer sea temperatures tend to increase windshear, leading to fewer storms overall. When big storms do form, meanwhile, they churn up cooler water from beneath the surface, which also tends to tamp down nascent storms that might otherwise form.

A Dangerous Future

These results are bad news because stronger storms are far more dangerous than weaker ones. A 2005 study that examined hurricane impacts from 1900 to 2005 found that Category 4 and 5 storms accounted for only 6% of U.S. landfalls, but caused 48% of all hurricane damage. Using this study as a starting point, and accounting for the projected mix of more bigger storms and fewer smaller ones, Knutson's team estimated that by 2100, the overall destructive potential of hurricanes may increase by 30%.

Hurricanes do most of their damage with high winds and storm surges. The global warming effect on the former is debated, but the latter isn't. Global sea levels have risen approximately 1.7 mm per year between 1950 and 2009, and at an accelerated pace of 3.3 mm from 1993 on. This is due to climatic changes. Warmer water expands, melting ice puts more water in the ocean, and rainfall patterns have shifted. Sea level rise is worse in some places than others. As fate would have it, the Northeast Atlantic coast is one of those unfortunate locations. One recent study showed that sea levels from North Carolina to Canada have been rising at three to four times the global average since 1950. By definition, higher seas mean higher storm surges. This means that storms that might once not have caused a problem are getting more dangerous. And huge storms, whether amplified by global warming or not, can go from destructive to catastrophic. The danger is compounded by the fact that most coastal fortifications were built when sea levels were lower, on the assumption that conditions wouldn't change.

So whatever uncertainties exist about the role of global warming in hurricanes, the dangers storms pose are worsening. Meanwhile, improving observations and modeling will produce new insights into the relationship between climate and extreme weather. Sometimes, for instance, warming in one part of the world has unexpected effects in others.

Hurricane Sandy, for instance, might have headed out to sea were it not for a blocking ridge of high pressure to the north that guided it into a low pressure system moving eastward, creating a giant hybrid storm. One recent study suggests that such blocking highs may be related to melting ice in polar regions, which contributes to a "wavier" jet stream, the air current flowing from west to east across the Atlantic. "When the jet stream is in wavy configurations those waves tend to move eastward more slowly," says Jennifer Francis, a Rutgers climatologist and one of the authors. "All meteorologists know that the reason that's important is, those waves are what create our weather so it increases the chances of having a stuck weather pattern." Once "stuck," this pattern might lead to drought, more rainfall—or create a hurricane highway. We won't know the outcome for certain until it happens, but when it does, we had better be prepared.

Weird Weather Around the World Is Cause for Alarm

Christine Ottery

In this viewpoint, science and environment journalist and former Greenpeace Energydesk writer Christine Ottery explores examples of weird or extreme weather from recent years, the effects on the people who experienced them, and whether they can be linked to climate change.

As you read, consider the following questions:

1. What is the link between extreme heat waves and climate change?
2. How can a cold snap be related to a global warming trend?
3. What is the connection between flooding and climate change?

You've probably noticed there's been some weird stuff going on with the weather lately.

The sheer amount of different extreme weather events going on simultaneously around the world means this could be the winter when climate change becomes "real" in minds, after more than two decades of scientists telling us what its impacts would be.

The recent IPCC AR 5 report concluded the climate is changing and there is a 95% certainty that it is caused by our actions—

specifically the burning of fossil fuels, deforestation and land use change.

But the World Meteorological Organisation (WMO) told *Energydesk* "No single weather episode can prove or disprove global climate change." Right, and of course many complicated and interrelated variables are in play, of which climate change might only be one factor.

And yes, and there are problems with attributing specific weather to climate change until more sophisticated reverse modeling is possible—an issue examined in a 2013 modeling paper identifying the contribution of climate change for some major flooding and storm events in 2012.

But that does not mean the question should not be asked. As Bob Ward from Grantham Research Institute on Climate Change and the Environment at LSE told *Energydesk*: "The right question is not 'was it caused by climate change?' But 'what impact has climate change had on it?'" He added: "It would be unlikely an almost 1 degree increase in global temperature would have no part to play in extreme weather events."

What Ward and a group of scientists around the world seem to be saying is that the weather events this winter fit into weather patterns and trends that are consistent with the basic physics of climate change.

For instance, the WMO said: "We do expect to see an increase in extreme heat and precipitation. Already dry regions are expected to become drier and wet ones wetter under IPCC scenarios."

Energydesk took a look at the most recent evidence on the links between climate change and the types of events we've experienced this winter and attempted to unpick how strong these are.

1. Australia's Heatwaves

What's happening?

Last year was Australia's hottest on record with temperatures 1.2 degrees above the average, a year in which Australia's Bureau of Meteorology had to add a new colour to its maps to represent new extremes in heat.

In December 2013 extreme heat developed over southern, central and eastern Australia, with especially high temperatures in the Australian interior into the new year, according to the bureau.

What does this mean for people?

A litany of issues: 100 blazes burning in South Australia, Victoria and New South Wales, New South Wales and Queensland are suffering drought, heart attacks surged 300% during the heatwave, a spike in deaths in Victoria, blackouts, the Australian Open had to stop play after tennis players collapsed.

What's the science say about links between heatwaves and climate change?

Essentially, the climate in Australia has warmed by about a degree since 1950, and the off-the-charts heatwaves of 2013 is in line with this trend say government meterologists. Average temperatures are projected to be one to five degrees C more by 2070.

The link between climate change and record heatwaves is clear, according to Australian scientists at the Climate Council—they created the body after the Australian Climate Commission was unceremoniously axed by PM Tony Abbott's government.

The council also says climate change is increasing the risk of bushfires.

Scientist says...

Peter Stott, head of climate monitoring at the UK Meteorological Office Hadley Centre told the FT: "Rising temperatures in Australia are a signal of climate change that has emerged very clearly from recent analysis. Last year's temperatures were a long way outside the envelope of variability that we would expect in the absence of climate change."

Where else in the world?

Argentina has also witnessed one of the worst heatwaves on record at the end of December, according to the WMO. Extreme warmth settled over Russia towards the end of 2013, according to NOAA.

2. UK flooding & storms

What's happening?

The UK has been battered by one storm after another since the start of December, with a series of storms tracking in off the Atlantic bringing strong winds and heavy rain.

According to the MET office December and January's rainfall was "one of, if not the most, exceptional periods of winter rainfall in the last 248 years."

PM David Cameron not only put his wellies on for a photo op but said he "strongly suspects" the climate change is causing more "abnormal weather events" such as the floods the UK has been seeing this winter. Even Princes William and Harry have been lugging sandbags.

The British Geological Survey warned that floods could last for months in some areas.

What does this mean for people?

Nearly 6,000 homes flooded across the UK, tens of thousands without electricity, rail networks disrupted, cost of the cleanup could be £1bn to £3bn depending on duration.

What does the science say about the link with the flooding and climate change?

What we can say is that it doesn't look like a coincidence that four of the five wettest years recorded in the UK have happened since 2000 at the same time as have also had the seven warmest years. As the Met Office pointed out in its recent report, there is an increasing evidence showing heavy rainfall is becoming heavier. They say this is consistent with what you'd expect from basic physics; the atmosphere in a warmer world holds more water vapour = more intense downpours.

The Met office also linked the UK's storminess with an erratic jet stream—the belt of strong winds circling the planet—over the Pacific Ocean and North America. The North Atlantic jet stream, which blows in storms from the west towards the UK, has been 30% stronger than normal, which links to to exceptional wind patterns in the stratosphere with a very intense

Polar Vortex—which has also been affecting weather in the US and Canada.

This whole process was driven by higher than normal ocean temperatures in the West Pacific that was most probably linked to climate change.

Scientist says...

Professor Myles Allen, University of Oxford, said: "There are simple physical reasons, supported by computer modelling of similar events back in the 2000s, to suspect that human-induced warming of the climate system has increased the risk of the kind of heavy rainfall events that are playing a major role in these floods."

Where else in the world?

In December Brazil saw torrential rains that saw at least 22 people killed and tens of thousands made homeless.

3. US & Canada cold snap

What's happening?

Extremely cold weather in the US and Canada over the past couple of months—even the Niagara Falls froze. The pattern established in December has continued till mid-February, says the WMO.

In an unprecedented move, the White House released a video explaining how the freezing spell was linked to climate change. The White House also organised a Google+ hangout on the Polar Vortex phenomenon.

What does it mean for people?

The freezing weather left around 21 people dead, cancelled 4,000 flights in one day causing traffic chaos across the country and costing the economy an estimated $5bn.

What does the science say about the link with the cold snap and climate change?

It might seem counter-intuitive, but the cold snap is likely to be linked to climate change.

A split between the Pacific and Atlantic jet streams—with its root in warming ocean temperatures in the Pacific—has resulted in colder air being carried south over North America.

Warming sea ice has also been involved in the frigid weather according to recent studies. It has been implicated in a huge meander in the jet stream over North America resulting in warm weather over Alaska and the west of the US while the rest of the US and Canada freezes.

Another theory about melting Arctic ice driving weather changes is the "Arctic Paradox" or "Warm Arctic–Cold Continent" pattern. Research suggests that as more Arctic sea ice is melting in the summer, the Arctic Ocean warms and radiates heat into the back into the atmosphere in winter.

This disturbs the Polar Vortex—essentially a pattern of strong winds circulating around a low-pressure system that normally sits over the Arctic in the winter—bringing relatively mild conditions to the Arctic while places far to the south bear the brunt of freezing winds. The Polar Vortex is stronger than normal, with increased winds around the vortex, and the vortex has distorted and its core has extended down over Canada.

Scientist says...

In the White House video, President Obama's science and technology advisor, Dr John Holdren, said: "A growing body of evidence suggests that the kind of extreme cold experienced by the United States is a pattern we can expect to see with increasing frequency as global warming continues.

"I believe the odds are that we can expect as a result of global warming to see more of this pattern of extreme cold in the mid latitudes and some extreme warm in the far north."

4. Supertyphoon Haiyan

What happened?

Hitting the Philippines with winds of 310km/h, typhoon Haiyan was the strongest tropical cyclone to make landfall in recorded history. The devastation in coastal areas such as Tacloban was principally caused by a six-metre storm surge that carried away even concrete buildings.

What did it mean for people?

Haiyan killed 5,000 people, flattened islands and damaged more than a million houses. Humanitarian disaster.

What does the science say about the link with supertyphoon and climate change?

There's a lot of discussion among scientists over whether storms are getting worse in a warming world. Meteorologists say it's impossible to blame climate change for individual storms.

Scientists think it's plausible that tropical storm activity will rise as the planet warms, on balance. This is despite the effects of increasingly strong 'shearing' winds to prevent the formation of storms or dissipate them.

There is some evidence linking climate change to increasing storm intensity over the past three decades, especially in north Atlantic where data is available, as described in the IPCC 5 report. But in other places, such as the northwest Pacific basin, our knowledge is more sketchy because of a lack of data.

One factor in the destruction Haiyan reaped that could be linked to climate change is the fact that rising sea levels, caused by global warming, contributed to the volume of water of the storm surge.

Scientist says...

Julian Heming, a tropical storm prediction scientist at the Met Office told The Telegraph: "We need to look at long-term climate models before we can be certain. But the indications are that the frequency of the storms may decrease—but their intensity will increase."

Where else in the world?

Climate change was linked to Hurricane Sandy, which hit the east coast of the US in October 2013. The storm was exacerbated by a "blocking high" of cold air coming down from Canada, a phenomenon linked to global warming by climate scientists.

Periodical and Internet Sources Bibliography

The following articles have been selected to supplement the diverse views presented in this chapter.

Sterling Burnett, "Neither Rising Sea Levels Nor Extreme Weather Getting Worse," Climate Change Dispatch, March 28, 2016. http://climatechangedispatch.com/neither-rising-sea-levels-nor -extreme-weather-getting-worse.

John Carey, "Global Warming and the Science of Extreme Weather," *Scientific American*, June 29, 2011.

GlobalChange.gov, "Extreme Weather." http://nca2014.globalchange .gov/highlights/report-findings/extreme-weather.

Marlowe Hood, "Climate Change Making Extreme Weather Events Worse: UN," Physics.org, November 8, 2016. https://phys.org /news/2016-11-climate-extreme-weather-events-worse.html.

M. J. Kelly, "Trends in Extreme Weather Events since 1900—An Enduring Conundrum for Wise Policy Advice," *Journal of Geography & Natural Disasters*, February 17, 2016.

Marc Morano, "'Floods Are Not Increasing': Dr. Roger Pielke Jr. Slams 'Global Warming' Link to Floods & Extreme Weather—How Does Media 'Get Away with This?'" Climate Depot, August 23, 2016. http://www.climatedepot.com/2016/08/23/floods-are -not-increasing-dr-roger-pielke-jr-slams-global-warming-link -to-floods-extreme-weather-how-does-media-get-away-with-this.

NASA, "The Impact of Climate Change on Natural Disasters," NASA. https://earthobservatory.nasa.gov/Features/RisingCost/rising_ cost5.php.

Fred Pearce, "El Niño and Climate Change: Wild Weather May Get Wilder," Yale Environment 360, February 11, 2016. http://e360 .yale.edu/features/el_nino_and_climate_change_wild_weather_ may_get_wilder.

Scientific American, "Why Global Warming Can Mean Harsher Winter Weather," *Scientific American*. https://www .scientificamerican.com/article/earthtalks-global-warming -harsher-winter.

US Environmental Protection Agency, "Understanding the Link Between Climate Change and Extreme Weather." https://www

.epa.gov/climate-change-science/understanding-link-between
-climate-change-and-extreme-weather.

John Vidal, "UK Floods and Extreme Global Weather Linked to El Niño and Climate Change," *The Guardian* (UK), December 27, 2015.

The Effects of Extreme Weather

Climate Has an Impact on Global Health

US Environmental Protection Agency

In the following viewpoint, the EPA explains the specific ways in which humans will be impacted by changing climate conditions and extreme weather. Factors like temperature, air quality, changes in ozone, and even the levels of allergens in the air will all affect quality of life. Extreme weather events will affect structures, services, and the incidents of disease, as well as mental health.

As you read, consider the following questions:

1. What populations are particularly likely to be affected by climate change?
2. How will air quality be affected?
3. What are vector-borne diseases?

Overview

The impacts of climate change include warming temperatures, changes in precipitation, increases in the frequency or intensity of some extreme weather events, and rising sea levels. These impacts threaten our health by affecting the food we eat, the water we drink, the air we breathe, and the weather we experience.

The severity of these health risks will depend on the ability of public health and safety systems to address or prepare for these changing threats, as well as factors such as an individual's behavior,

"Climate Impacts on Human Health," US Environmental Protection Agency, October 28, 2016.

age, gender, and economic status. Impacts will vary based on a where a person lives, how sensitive they are to health threats, how much they are exposed to climate change impacts, and how well they and their community are able to adapt to change.

People in developing countries may be the most vulnerable to health risks globally, but climate change poses significant threats to health even in wealthy nations such as the United States. Certain populations, such as children, pregnant women, older adults, and people with low incomes, face increased risks; see the section below on Populations of Concern.

Temperature-Related Impacts

Warmer average temperatures will lead to hotter days and more frequent and longer heat waves.[2] These changes will lead to an increase in heat-related deaths in the United States—reaching as much as thousands to tens of thousands of additional deaths each year by the end of the century during summer months.

These deaths will not be offset by the smaller reduction in cold-related deaths projected in the winter months. However, adaptive responses, such as wider use of air conditioning, are expected to reduce the projected increases in death from extreme heat.[1]

Exposure to extreme heat can lead to heat stroke and dehydration, as well as cardiovascular, respiratory, and cerebrovascular disease.[3] [4] Excessive heat is more likely to affect populations in northern latitudes where people are less prepared to cope with excessive temperatures. Certain types of populations are more vulnerable than others: for example, outdoor workers, student athletes, and homeless people tend to be more exposed to extreme heat because they spend more time outdoors. Low-income households and older adults may lack access to air conditioning which also increases exposure to extreme heat. Additionally, young children, pregnant women, older adults, and people with certain medical conditions are less able to regulate their body temperature and can therefore be more vulnerable to extreme heat.[1]

Urban areas are typically warmer than their rural surroundings. Large metropolitan areas such as St. Louis, Philadelphia, Chicago, and Cincinnati have seen notable increases in death rates during heat waves.[2] Climate change is projected to increase the vulnerability of urban populations to heat-related health impacts in the future. Heat waves are also often accompanied by periods of stagnant air, leading to increases in air pollution and associated health effects.[2]

Air Quality Impacts

Changes in the climate affect the air we breathe both indoors and outdoors. Warmer temperatures and shifting weather patterns can worsen air quality, which can lead to asthma attacks and other respiratory and cardiovascular health effects.[1] Wildfires, which are expected to continue to increase in number and severity as the climate changes, create smoke and other unhealthy air pollutants.[1] Rising carbon dioxide levels and warmer temperatures also affect airborne allergens, such as ragweed pollen.

Despite significant improvements in U.S. air quality since the 1970s, as of 2014 about 57 million Americans lived in counties that did not meet national air quality standards.[5] Climate change may make it even harder for states to meet these standards in the future, exposing more people to unhealthy air.

Increases in ozone

Scientists project that warmer temperatures from climate change will increase the frequency of days with unhealthy levels of ground-level ozone, a harmful air pollutant, and a component in smog.[1]

- People exposed to higher levels of ground-level ozone are at greater risk of dying prematurely or being admitted to the hospital for respiratory problems.[1]

- Ground-level ozone can damage lung tissue, reduce lung function, and inflame airways. This can aggravate asthma or other lung diseases. Children, older adults, outdoor workers, and those with asthma and other chronic lung diseases are particularly at risk.[5]

- Because warm, stagnant air tends to increase the formation of ozone, climate change is likely to increase levels of ground-level ozone in already-polluted areas of the United States and increase the number of days with poor air quality.[1]

- The higher concentrations of ozone due to climate change may result in tens to thousands of additional ozone-related illnesses and premature deaths per year by 2030 in the United States, assuming no change in projected air quality policies.[1]

Changes in particulate matter

Particulate matter is the term for a category of extremely small particles and liquid droplets suspended in the atmosphere. Fine particles include those smaller than 2.5 micrometers (about one ten-thousandth of an inch). Some particulate matter such as dust, wildfire smoke, and sea spray occur naturally, while some is created by human activities such as the burning of fossil fuels to produce energy. These particles may be emitted directly or may be formed in the atmosphere from chemical reactions of gases such as sulfur dioxide, nitrogen dioxide, and volatile organic compounds.

- Inhaling fine particles can lead to a broad range of adverse health effects, including lung cancer, chronic obstructive pulmonary disease (COPD), and cardiovascular disease.[1]

- Climate change is expected to increase the number and severity of wildfires. Particulate matter from wildfire smoke can often be carried very long distances by the wind, affecting people who live far from the source of this air pollutant.

- Older adults are particularly sensitive to short-term particle exposure, with a higher risk of hospitalization and death.[1] Outdoor workers like firefighters can also have high exposure.

Due to the complex factors that influence atmospheric levels of fine particulate matter, scientists do not yet know whether climate change will increase or decrease particulate matter concentrations across the United States.[167] Particulate matter can be removed from the air by rainfall, and precipitation is expected to increase in quantity though not necessarily frequency. Climate-related changes in stagnant air episodes, wind patterns, emissions from vegetation and the chemistry of atmospheric pollutants will also affect particulate matter levels.[1]

Changes in allergens and asthma triggers
Allergic illnesses, including hay fever, affect about one-third of the U.S. population, and more than 34 million Americans have been diagnosed with asthma.[1] Climate change may affect allergies and respiratory health.[1] The spring pollen season is already occurring earlier in the United States for certain types of plants, and the length of the season has increased for some plants with highly allergenic pollen such as ragweed.[1] In addition to lengthening the ragweed pollen season, rising carbon dioxide concentrations and temperatures may also lead to earlier flowering, more flowers, and increased pollen levels in ragweed.[14]

Impacts from Extreme Weather Events

Increases in the frequency or severity of some extreme weather events, such as extreme precipitation, flooding, droughts, and storms, threaten the health of people during and after the event.[1] The people most at risk include young children, older adults, people with disabilities or medical conditions, and the poor. Extreme events can affect human health in a number of ways by:

- Reducing the availability of safe food and drinking water.[1]

- Damaging roads and bridges, disrupting access to hospitals and pharmacies.[1]

- Interrupting communication, utility, and health care services.[1]

- Contributing to carbon monoxide poisoning from improper use of portable electric generators during and after storms[.1]

- Increasing stomach and intestinal illness, particularly following power outages.[1]

- Creating or worsening mental health impacts such as depression and post-traumatic stress disorder (PTSD).[1]

In addition, emergency evacuations pose health risks to older adults, especially those with limited mobility who cannot use elevators during power outages. Evacuations may be complicated by the need for concurrent transfer of medical records, medications, and medical equipment. Some individuals with disabilities may also be disproportionally affected if they are unable to access evacuation routes, have difficulty in understanding or receiving warnings of impending danger, or have limited ability to communicate their needs.

Vectorborne Diseases

Vectorborne diseases are illnesses that are transmitted by disease vectors, which include mosquitoes, ticks, and fleas. These vectors can carry infectious pathogens, such as viruses, bacteria, and protozoa, from animals to humans. Changes in temperature, precipitation, and extreme events increases the geographic range of diseases spread by vectors and can lead to illnesses occurring earlier in the year.

The geographic range of ticks that carry Lyme disease is limited by temperature. As air temperatures rise, ticks are likely to become active earlier in the season, and their range is likely to continue to expand northward.[1] Typical symptoms of Lyme disease include fever, headache, fatigue, and a characteristic skin rash.

Mosquitoes thrive in certain climate conditions and can spread diseases like West Nile virus. Extreme temperatures—too cold, hot, wet, or dry—influence the location and number of mosquitoes that transmit West Nile virus. More than three million people were estimated to be infected with West Nile virus in the United States from 1999 to 2010.[1]

The spread of climate-sensitive diseases will depend on both climate and non-climate factors such as land use, socioeconomic and cultural conditions, pest control, access to health care, and human responses to disease risk. The United States has public health infrastructure and programs to monitor, manage, and prevent the spread of many diseases. The risks for climate-sensitive diseases can be much higher in poorer countries that have less capacity to prevent and treat illness.[8]

Water-Related Illnesses

People can become ill if exposed to contaminated drinking or recreational water. Climate change increases the risk of illness through increasing temperature, more frequent heavy rains and runoff, and the effects of storms. Health impacts may include gastrointestinal illness like diarrhea, effects on the body's nervous and respiratory systems, or liver and kidney damage.[1]

- Climate impacts can affect exposure to waterborne pathogens (bacteria, viruses, and parasites such as *Cryptosporidium* and *Giardia*); toxins produced by harmful algal and cyanobacterial blooms in the water; and chemicals that end up in water from human activities.[1]

- Changing water temperatures mean that waterborne *Vibrio* bacteria and harmful algal toxins will be present in the water or in seafood at different times of the year, or in places where they were not previously threats.[1]

- Runoff and flooding resulting from increases in extreme precipitation, hurricane rainfall, and storm surge will increasingly contaminate water bodies used for recreation (such as lakes and beaches), shellfish harvesting waters, and sources of drinking water.[1]

- Extreme weather events and storm surges can damage or exceed the capacity of water infrastructure (such as drinking water or wastewater treatment plants), increasing the risk that people will be exposed to contaminants.[1]

Water resource, public health, and environmental agencies in the United States provide many public health safeguards to reduce risk of exposure and illness even if water becomes contaminated.

These include water quality monitoring, drinking water treatment standards and practices, beach closures, and issuing advisories for boiling drinking water and harvesting shellfish.

Food Safety and Nutrition

Climate change and the direct impacts of higher concentrations of carbon dioxide in the atmosphere are expected to affect food safety and nutrition.[1] Extreme weather events can also disrupt or slow the distribution of food.[1]

- Higher air temperatures can increase cases of *Salmonella* and other bacteria-related food poisoning because bacteria grow more rapidly in warm environments. These diseases can cause gastrointestinal distress and, in severe cases, death.[1] Practices to safeguard food can help avoid these illnesses even as the climate changes.

- Climate change will have a variety of impacts that may increase the risk of exposure to chemical contaminants in food. For example, higher sea surface temperatures will lead to higher mercury concentrations in seafood, and increases in extreme weather events will introduce contaminants into the food chain through stormwater runoff.[1]

- Higher concentrations of carbon dioxide in the air can act as a "fertilizer" for some plants, but lowers the levels of protein and essential minerals in crops such as wheat, rice, and potatoes, making these foods less nutritious.[1]

- Extreme events, such as flooding and drought, create challenges for food distribution if roads and waterways are damaged or made inaccessible.

Mental Health

Any changes in a person's physical health or surrounding environment can also have serious impacts on their mental health. In particular, experiencing an extreme weather event can cause stress and other mental health consequences, particularly when a person loses loved ones or their home.[1]

- Individuals with mental illness are especially vulnerable to extreme heat; studies have found that having a pre-existing mental illness tripled the risk of death during heat waves.[1] People taking medication for mental illness that makes it difficult to regulate their body temperature are particularly at risk.

- Even the perceived threat of climate change (for example from reading or watching news reports about climate change) can influence stress responses and mental health.[1]

- Some groups of people are at higher risk for mental health impacts, such as children and older adults, pregnant and post-partum women, people with pre-existing mental illness (see above), people with low incomes, and emergency workers.[1]

Populations of Concern

Some groups of people are more vulnerable than others to health risks from climate change.[1] Three factors contribute to vulnerability: *sensitivity*, which refers to the degree to which people or groups are affected by a stressor such as higher temperatures; *exposure*, which refers to physical contact between a person and a stressor; and *adaptive capacity*, which refers to an ability to adjust to or avoid potential hazards. For example, while older adults are sensitive to extreme heat, an older person living in an air-conditioned apartment won't be exposed as long as she stays indoors, and as long as she can afford to pay for the electricity to run the air conditioner. Her ability take these actions is a measure of her adaptive capacity.

Some populations are especially vulnerable to climate health risks due to particular sensitivities, high likelihood of exposure, low adaptive capacity, or combinations of these factors.

- Communities of color (including Indigenous communities as well as specific racial and ethnic groups), low income, immigrants, and limited English proficiency face disproportionate vulnerabilities due to a wide variety of factors, such as higher risk of exposure, socioeconomic and educational factors that affect their adaptive capacity, and a higher prevalence of medical conditions that affect their sensitivity.[1]

- Children are vulnerable to many health risks due to biological sensitivities and more opportunities for exposure (due to activities such as playing outdoors). Pregnant women are vulnerable to heat waves and other extreme events, like flooding.[1]

- Older adults are vulnerable to many of the impacts of climate change. They may have greater sensitivity to heat and contaminants, a higher prevalence of disability or preexisting medical conditions, or limited financial resources that make it difficult to adapt to impacts.[1]

- Occupational groups, such as outdoor workers, paramedics, firefighters, and transportation workers, as well as workers in hot indoor work environments, will be especially vulnerable to extreme heat and exposure to vectorborne diseases.[1]

- People with disabilities can be very vulnerable during extreme weather events, unless communities ensure that their emergency response plans specifically accommodate them.

- People with chronic medical conditions are typically vulnerable to extreme heat, especially if they are taking medications that make it difficult to regulate body temperature.[1] Power outages can be particularly threatening for people reliant on certain medical equipment.

Other Health Impacts

Other linkages exist between climate change and human health. For example, changes in temperature and precipitation, as well as droughts and floods, will affect agricultural yields and production.[9] In some regions of the world, these impacts may compromise food security and threaten human health through malnutrition, the spread of infectious diseases, and food poisoning. The worst of these effects are projected to occur in developing countries, among vulnerable populations.[8] Declines in human health in other countries can affect the United States through trade, migration, and immigration and has implications for national security.[14]

Although the impacts of climate change have the potential to affect human health in the United States and around the world, there is a lot we can do to prepare for and adapt to these changes—such as establishing early warning systems for heat waves and other extreme events, taking steps to reduce vulnerabilities among populations of concern, raising awareness among healthcare professionals, and ensuring that infrastructure is built to accommodate anticipated future changes in climate. Understanding the threats that climate change poses to human health is the first step in working together to lower risks and be prepared.

References

1. USGCRP (2016). *Impacts of Climate Change on Human Health in the United States: A Scientific Assessment.* Crimmins, A., J. Balbus, J.L. Gamble, C.B. Beard, J.E. Bell, D. Dodgen, R.J. Eisen, N.Fann, M.D. Hawkins, S.C. Herring, L. Jantarasami, D.M. Mills, S. Saha, M.C. Sarofim, J.Trtanj, and L.Ziska, Eds. U.S. Global Change Research Program, Washington, DC. 312 pp. dx.doi.org/10.7930/J0R49NQX.

2. USGCRP (2016). Luber, G., K. Knowlton, J. Balbus, H. Frumkin, M. Hayden, J. Hess, M. McGeehin, N. Sheats, L. Backer, C. B. Beard, K. L. Ebi, E. Maibach, R. S. Ostfeld, C. Wiedinmyer, E. Zielinski-Gutiérrez, and L. Ziska, 2014: *Ch. 9: Human Health. Climate Change Impacts in the United States: The Third National Climate Assessment,* J. M. Melillo, Terese (T.C.) Richmond, and G. W. Yohe, Eds., U.S. Global Change Research Program, 220-256. doi:10.7930/J0PN93H5.

3. USGCRP (2009). *Global Climate Change Impacts in the United States.* Karl, T.R., J.M. Melillo, and T.C. Peterson (eds.). United States Global Change Research Program. Cambridge University Press, New York, NY, USA.

4. CCSP (2008). *Analyses of the effects of global change on human health and welfare and human systems.* A Report by the U.S. Climate Change Science Program and the Subcommittee on Global Change Research. Gamble, J.L. (ed.), K.L. Ebi, F.G. Sussman, T.J. Wilbanks, (Authors). U.S. Environmental Protection Agency, Washington, DC, USA.

5. EPA (2014). Air Quality Trends. Accessed March 1, 2016.

6. NRC (2010). *Advancing the Science of Climate Change.* National Research Council. The National Academies Press, Washington, DC, USA.

7. EPA (2009). *Assessment of the Impacts of Global Change on Regional U.S. Air Quality: A Synthesis of Climate Change Impacts on Ground-Level Ozone (An Interim Report of the U.S. EPA Global Change Research Program).* U.S. Environmental Protection Agency, Washington, DC, USA.

8. IPCC (2014). *Climate Change 2014: Synthesis Report.* Contribution of Working Groups I, II and III to the Fifth Assessment Report of the Intergovernmental Panel on Climate Change [Core Writing Team, R.K. Pachauri and L.A. Meyer (eds.)]. IPCC, Geneva, Switzerland, 151 p. (PDF, 80 pp, 4.6MB).

9. USDA (2015). *Climate Change, Global Food Security, and the U.S. Food System.* Brown, M.E., J.M. Antle, P. Backlund, E.R. Carr, W.E. Easterling, M.K. Walsh, C. Ammann, W. Attavanich, C.B. Barrett, M.F. Bellemare, V. Dancheck, C. Funk, K. Grace, J.S.I. Ingram, H. Jiang, H. Maletta, T. Mata, A. Murray, M. Ngugi, D. Ojima, B. O'Neill, and C. Tebaldi, 146 p.

Animal Populations Are Affected by Climate Upheaval

Juan Lubroth

There has been much attention given to how people will be affected by extreme weather and climate change. The following viewpoint from the Food and Agriculture Organization of the United Nations explores how these situations will affect animals and what needs to be done to address both the risks and the possible outcomes.

As you read, consider the following questions:

1. How does climate change affect the transmission of diseases in animals?
2. How will farming practices need to change?
3. What is meant by preventative veterinary medicine?

Introduction

Systematic reviews of empirical studies provide the best evidence for the relationships between the health of humans, animals and plants, and weather or climate factors. Regarding the public health sector, Chapter 8 of the Working Group II report of the Intergovernmental Panel on Climate Change (IPCC) for 2007 comprises an update on the state of knowledge of the associations between weather/climatic factors and public health outcomes for human populations concerned (Patz et al., 2005). Direct exposure to climate change

Source: Food and Agriculture Organization of the United Nations, Juan Lubroth, Climate change and animal health, http://www.fao.org/docrep/017/i3084e/i3084e05.pdf. Reproduced with permission.

comprises changing weather patterns (increasing temperatures, more precipitation, rising sea-level and more frequent extreme events). Indirect exposure comprises changes in water, air and food quality, vector ecology and changes in ecosystems, agriculture, industry and settlements. Additional indirect exposure may result from social and economic disruption. Possibilities for adaptation extend to concurrent direct-acting and modifying (conditioning) influences of environmental, social and health system factors. How critical global warming could become a threat to public health has been studied for several risk settings, comprising malaria, water shortage, famines and coastal flooding. Water shortage is often associated with unsanitary water conditions and therefore with a major impact of climate change on health, for example, through diarrhoeal disease.

Unfortunately, in the animal health realms, comprehensive, formal reviews are rare (de la Rocque, Rioux and Slingenbergh, 2008). Climate change and general anthropogenic factors together alter both the farming and the natural landscapes and in the process impact the health of animals in multiple ways. This paper is primarily concerned with the effects of climate change on disease ecology and transmission dynamics. Importantly, changes in host distribution, density and their availability to existing pathogens may translate in disease emergence in animals and at the animal-human interface. A pathogen may: (i) find access to new territories and host landscapes; or (ii) turn more host aggressive in settings where the hosts have become more abundant and/or immune-compromised; or (iii) perform a host species jump, possibly in response to enhance host species mixing or contacts. Geographic spread or invasion may entail a range expansion or, in case of saltation dispersal, kick-start a complete pathogen genetic remake. The disease emergence category featuring an expansion of the geographic range is both relatively common and also more likely to be affected by climate change, and for this reason is the main focus of this paper. This group of disease complexes comprises insect pests, ecto-parasites, endo-parasites, arthropod-borne disease complexes and pathogens carried by foods and fomites. A set of global factors is believed to drive a worldwide redistribution of hosts, vectors and pathogens. Climate change clearly plays a role in this regard, enhancing or decreasing the introduction and invasions of disease agents, even when primarily caused by other factors such as the demography of humans and animals, encroachment of the natural resource base, land use, agriculture, the greater mobility of people, and the enhanced trade and traffic volumes. When it comes to the role of climate change in disease ecology and pathogen evolution, there is a need to duly consider the collective host–pathogen–environment interplay. In a stable environment, a situation of relative evolutionary stasis, host–pathogen–environment complexes tend to become more entrenched, with location-bound pathogen traits selected for. Conversely, in a rapidly changing environment, it is pathogen opportunism and generalist type versatility that matters.

Climate Change and Transmission Ecology

From a climate change perspective, it is important to assess the extent to which a pathogenic agent is exposed to the conditions outside the host body. A free-living pathogen stage plays a role even in the direct transmission of respiratory diseases. The survival of the common flu virus on doorknobs or during aero-gene transmission or by means of handshakes is influenced by ambient temperature and humidity (Lowen et al., 2007). The role of environmental pathogen load is perhaps more obvious still in the case of faecal-oral or water-borne transmission. Food poisoning usually entails faecal contamination of food items. Environmental robustness is a prominent feature in certain stages of the life history of larger parasites, including in nematodes, with larvae surviving for weeks or more outside the host on pastures. The natural cycle of avian influenza viruses in mallard ducks, its foremost natural host, involves ingestion of water containing the virus. Natural avian influenza virus replication occurs mainly in the distal end of the enteric duck tract (Jourdain et al., 2010). Viruses deposited by migratory waterfowl during summer breeding at higher latitudes may be stored in permafrost conditions in subarctic regions and survive for centuries (Zhang et al., 2006). Likewise does the anaerobe *Bacillus anthrax* bacterium survive for decades in the form of spores in the soil (Dragon and Rennie, 1995).

Disease agents transmitted by arthropods form a distinct, albeit related category. Indirect transmission of protozoan disease agents may be facilitated by three-host ticks. Soft ticks feeding on warthogs play a role in the transmission of African swine fever (ASF) (Kleiboeker and Scoles, 2001). The causative agent of ASF, a DNA virus, may survive for eight years in the tick vector. There are also a number of midge- or mosquito-borne disease complexes that involve a dormant pathogen stage. For example, Rift Valley fever (RVF) virus may survive in mosquito eggs for years, until a prolonged heavy rainfall facilitates an awakening of Aedes mosquitoes, feeding on ruminants and thus kick-starting a RVF outbreak (Mondet et al., 2005; Anyamba et al., 2009). Infected ruminants that end up in densely populated irrigation schemes may also attract mosquitoes feeding on humans and thus contribute to the transmission of RVF among humans.

Midges are sometimes blown by wind across wider geographic areas. This is probably what happened with bluetongue virus (BTV8) introduction in the United Kingdom, in the summer of 2006, after the virus had first spread westwards across Belgium (Gloster et al., 2008). It is very possible that also the flare up of the Schmallenberg virus (SBV) in the United Kingdom in early 2012 resulted from wind-carried infected midges arriving from mainland Europe (Gibbens, 2012).

In the direct-indirect transmission spectrum, directly, swiftly transmitted common flu, short-lived fevers, faecal–oral, food and vector-borne transmission to more prominent free-living parasite stage can be noted. In this regard, ecto-parasites and myiasis-causing insects should also be considered. Arthropod pests are strongly modulated by climatic and weather conditions. For example, both the Old World screwworm fly (OWS), *Chrysomya bezziana*, and the New World screwworm fly, *Cochliomyia hominivorax*, feature a prominent free-living stage. The adult female fly deposits eggs in open wounds and also minor skin lesions or on mucous membranes, providing access for the evolving larval stages to life tissue of warm blooded hosts (Spradbery, 1991). The latter is obligatory for this life cycle stage. Hundreds of larvae may result from a single egg batch, producing an ever-larger wound. Additional screwworm flies are lured to the scene, and death of the affected host may eventually result. The larvae leaving the wound fall to the soil and bury themselves 2 cm deep, to turn into a pupa for about a period of one week until a new fly emerges. Adult flies feed on nectar and rely on adequate vegetation.

...Substantial areas of the Arabian Peninsula today provide suitable conditions for OWS persistence. OWS flare-up in the Gulf countries has been reported since the 1980s. Apart from rather small foci in Oman, Saudi Arabia and Iran, OWS myiasis did not pose a serious problem to livestock production until a major outbreak erupted in the mid-1990s in Iraq. As a result of the United Nations sanctions, the country ran out of acaracide supplies required to keep the sheep flocks free from ticks. With the higher number of skin lesions, also the vulnerability to OWS incursions increased. An FAO study predicted OWS suitability across the Arabian Peninsula on the basis of satellite-derived proxies for soil temperature and presence of vegetation. The results suggested Yemen as a potential area where OWS might flare-up and turn endemic. Indeed, large areas of southwestern Yemen have turned OWS endemic during the 2000s, with ever prominent, mostly springtime, disease outbreaks.

The effects of climate change on tsetse flies, the vector of human and animal African trypanosomiases, is rather different, despite certain similarities between the tsetse and the screwworm fly life history. The tsetse fly also features a pupal stage in the soil. However, whereas a single screwworm fly egg batch may yield over 200 larvae, the female tsetse fly produces only one larva every nine days. During its total lifespan, a female tsetse fly may produce six to eight larvae, each of which undergo a pupal development period of about three weeks depending on ambient temperatures (Ford, 1971). Unlike screwworm flies, dispersing over hundreds of kilometres within weeks, tsetse flies sit and wait for the host to show up. Tsetse fly activity is restricted to 15 to 20 minutes a day.

From the above examples, it becomes clear that the effects of climate change on disease complexes may take many different forms, complicating comparison and generalization. Whereas the tsetse fly distribution in Ethiopia entails a gradual encroachment of the country's central highland plateau (Slingenbergh, 1992.), recorded since the 1960s, the Old World Screwworm fly rather abruptly colonized the Arabian peninsula, first the Mesopotamia valley in Iraq and later parts of Yemen, within the course of just two decades (Siddig et al., 2005).

A disease complex may also change the transmission mode or pattern. For example, ASF virus circulates in the form of at least 22 different genotypes in its sylvatic cycle—the warthogs as distributed in the miombo woodlands of southern Africa. Yet, in 2007, genotype II found its way to central Europe, starting in Georgia, in a Black Sea port. It is believed that meat products containing ASF virus were shipped from Mozambique or Madagascar and disposed of in Georgia as food scraps and fed to local pigs. Today ASF is progressively colonizing higher latitude areas of eastern Europe, propagated by people transporting contaminated pig meat products, through pig production, and also involving the Eurasian wild boar, *Sus scrofa*.

Resilience in Animal Health

Basically, there are three distinct entry points that may lead to a better way of coping with the negative consequences of climate change and associated drivers of disease, pest dynamics and the overall health status of animals.

Preventive veterinary medicine

As has been shown by the FAO Emergency Prevention System (EMPRES), since its creation in 1994, early warning, early detection, and early response have been key to the prevention and control of both old and new pests and diseases in animal and crop production. Prevention and curtailing the spread of disease across country boundaries has become the credo of the FAO/World Organisation for Animal Health (OIE) initiative, Global Framework for the Progressive Control of Transboundary Animal Diseases (GF-TAD). Progressive control pathways and regional roadmaps are being designed to counter the spread of high-impact infectious livestock diseases such as foot-and-mouth disease (FMD), peste des petits ruminants (PPR) and ASF.

Early detection and early response were also key to the success of the Global Rinderpest Eradication Programme. Following years of vaccination of the entire national cattle herd, countries gradually replaced the blanket vaccination by early detection and early response, in the process consolidating and expanding the rinderpest-free areas. In mid-2011 both OIE and FAO proclaimed the world free from rinderpest.

Yet the flare-up of new disease and the persistence of chronic disease burden remain considerable, particularly in the developing world. Climate change-modulated vector-borne disease (VBD) complexes would appear to become more dynamic globally, especially in the temperate climate zones of the northern hemisphere. In many countries, the expertise in entomology and disease ecology within public veterinary services is inadequate to mount early warning and response mechanisms in the face of novel VBD emergencies. Improvements are required also in terms of a further integration of field veterinary work, laboratories and detection of critical control points further along the food chain.

A "One Health" approach conveniently deals with the collective risk factors acting at the level of natural and farming landscapes, on-farm, in slaughterhouses and processing and distribution circuits. "One Health" brings together health professionals engaged as veterinary practitioners and food inspectors, working in fisheries health, forestry, plant protection, natural resource management and, of course, food safety and public health.

Removing the divides separating today disciplines, sectors, institutions and political boundaries, undoing the compartmentalization as prevailing in government organizational structures, presents the major challenge under the "One Health" umbrella. For FAO, the "One Health" notion extends to the Food Chain Crisis Management Framework, a platform for all health professionals within the Organization (Tekola et al., 2012).

Adjustment of animal husbandry

Improvement in sanitation, hygiene or biosecurity may conveniently take a whole-of society approach. Risk factors vary with animal production subsectors and systems. The management of animal genetic resources, feeding practices, housing and bio-containment together play a key role in the maintenance of robust, healthy and productive animals. Agro-ecological resilience matters most where production environments reflect the local conditions. Local breeds may harbour genetic disease resistance and other traits reflecting their adjustment to the locally prevailing conditions.

Ruminant grazing in the open brings exposure to multiple arthropod-borne diseases. A growing armoury of quality vaccines is required to confront a vast array of old and new diseases. Vaccination is particularly a priority in developing countries. Disease flare-ups at the human-animal-ecosystems interfaces are particularly prominent in pig and poultry production, with Influenza A as a primary example. A number of new emerging diseases, in part climate change modulated, are finding their way from wildlife reservoirs via pigs to humans. Fruit bats may transmit Henipah viruses (HeV) or Reston Ebola virus (REBOV). The management of this growing number of veterinary and medical threats requires adjustment of natural resource management practices, land use and food and agriculture. Safe and healthy food and agriculture requires re-definition.

Social resilience

Empowering the community regarding health protection presents the key priority. With health systems and infrastructures being weakest in remote rural areas and harsh environments where ruminant livestock production is the most prominent among the prevailing farming systems, self-help options supported by community animal health outreach are rapidly gaining in importance. This extends to participatory disease surveillance and control, relying also on syndromic surveillance. Where vaccination is integrated with adjustments in husbandry and increased off-take results, prospects evolve for sustainable improvements in food and income security, in turn paving the way for an upgrading of the livestock production and farming systems in settings today featuring major disease burdens and low levels of productivity.

As the experience with rinderpest eradication has shown, community-based health protection efforts stand a good chance of success provided livelihood sustenance is made both the entry point and the ultimate rationale for the collective stakeholder efforts.

Conclusions

There has been a tendency to oversimplify the mechanisms by which climate change affects disease transmission and animal health status. Indeed, only a limited number of studies present validation of the direct effects of climate change itself. Climate change is to be considered in conjunction with the set of global factors today altering the earth terrestrial surface area and associated global biophysical systems.

The flare-up of novel pests and diseases of wildlife and livestock origin, and also the surge of food safety hazards, is likely to continue for decades to come. Risk analysis highlighting the implications of climate change in its broader context relies on the full consideration of the transmission ecology of pests and diseases. Transmission involving prominent free-living parasite stages is arguably more likely to be modulated by environmental factors including temperature, humidity and seasonality.

Risk management of emerging disease complexes in which climate change plays a role is best addressed under a "One Health" umbrella. For FAO, these efforts are centred around the collective biological risks in food production and supply chains.

References

Anyamba, A., Chretien, J-P, Small, J., Tucker, C.J., Formenty, P.B., Richardson, J.H., Britch, S.C., Schnabel, D.C., Erickson, R.L. & Linthicum, K.J. 2009. Prediction of a Rift Valley fever outbreak. *PNAS*, 106(3): 3955–959.

de la Rocque, S., Rioux, J.A. & Slingenbergh, J. 2008. Climate change: effects on animal disease systems and implications for surveillance and control. *Rev. sci. tech. Off. Int. Epiz,.* 27(2): 339–354.

Dragon, D.C. & Rennie, R.P. 1995. The ecology of anthrax spores: tough but not invincible. *Can. Vet. J.*, 36(5): 295–301.

Ford, J. 1971. *The role of the trypanosomiases in African ecology. A study of the tsetse fly problem.* New York, USA, and London, Oxford University Press.

Gibbens, N. 2012. Schmallenberg virus: a novel viral disease in northern Europe. *Veterinary Record*, 170.

Gilbert, M. & Slingenbergh, J. 2008. Geospatial demarcation of Old World Screwworm risk in the Middle East, an update. Rome, FAO.

Gloster, J., Burgin, L., Witham, C., Athanassiadou, M., Mets, F.R. & Mellor, Y.S. 2008. Bluetongue in the United Kingdom and northern Europe in 2007 and key issues for 2008. *Veterinary Record*, 162: 298–302.

Jourdain, E., Gunnarsson, G., Wahlgren, J., Latorre-Margalef, N., Bröjer, C. *et al.* 2010. Influenza virus in a natural host, the mallard: experimental infection data. *PLoS ONE*, 5(1): e.8935.

Kleiboeker, S.B. & Scoles, G.A. 2001. Pathogenesis of African swine fever virus in Ornithodoros ticks. *Animal Health Research Reviews*, 2: 121–128.

Lowen, A.C., Mubareka, S., Steel, J. & Palese P. 2007. Influenza virus transmission is dependent on relative humidity and temperature. *PLoS Pathog.*, 3(10): e151.

Mondet, B., Diaïte, A., Ndione J.A., Fall, A.G., Chevalier, V., Lancelot, R., Ndiaye, M. & Poncon, N. 2005. Rainfall patterns and population dynamics of *Aedes (Aedimorphus) vexans arabiensis*, Patton 1905 (Diptera: Culicidae), a potential vector of Rift Valley Fever virus in Senegal. *Journal of Vector Ecology*, 30(1): 102–106.

Patz, J.A., Campbell-Lendrum, D., Holloway, T. & Foley, J.A. 2005. Impact of regional climate change on human health. *Nature*, 438: 310–317.

Siddig, A., Al Jowary, S., Al Izzi, M., Hopkins, J., Hall, M.J.R & Slingenbergh, J. 2005. Seasonality of Old World screwworm myiasis in the Mesopotamia valley in Iraq. *Medical and Veterinary Entomology*, 19 (2): 140–150.

Slingenbergh, J. 1992. Tsetse control and agricultural development in Ethiopia. *World Animal Review*, 70–71: 30–36.

Spradbery, J.P. 1991. *A manual for the diagnosis of screw-worm fly.* Office of the Chief Veterinary Officer, Department of Agriculture, Fisheries and Forestry, Canberra, Australia.

Tekola, B., Lubroth, J., Slingenbergh, J., de Balogh, K., Morzaria, S., Newman, S., Subasinghe, R., El Idrissi, A., Ankers, P., Douglas, I., Kaeslin, E. & Poirson, J-M. 2012. The Food and Agriculture Organization (FAO) is advancing the One Health approach. *GRF One Health Summit* 2012. (unpublished). Rome, FAO.

Zhang, G., Shoham, D., Gilichinsky, D., Davydov, S., Castello, J.D. & Rogers, S.O. 2006. Evidence of Influenza A virus RNA in Siberian Lake ice. *J. Virol*, 24: 12229–12235.

Global Climate Risk Index 2015

- According to the Germanwatch Global Climate Risk Index, Honduras, Myanmar and Haiti were the countries affected most by extreme weather events between 1994 and 2013.

- Of the ten most affected countries (1994–2013), nine were developing countries in the low income or lower-middle income country group, while only one was classified an upper-middle income country.

- Altogether, more than 530,000 people died as a direct result of approx. 15,000 extreme weather events, and losses between 1994 and 2013 amounted to nearly 2.2 trillion USD (in Purchasing Power Parities).

- In 2013, the Philippines, Cambodia and India led the list of the most affected countries.

- The Fifth Assessment Report of the IPCC stresses that risks associated with extreme weather events will further increase with rising temperatures. Those risks are unevenly distributed, which is likely to worsen as a trend.

- Lima is a stepping-stone in the preparation of the Paris Agreement. Furthermore countries must make concrete decisions to advance the implementation of National Adaptation Plans, and to develop the work plan for the Warsaw International Mechanism to support countries in addressing climatic loss & damage.

- The year 2015 represents a paramount opportunity for the international community to advance policies and programmes that help reduce climatic losses. These are: the Paris Agreement that is expected to yield an universal climate regime (which comes into effect in 2020); the post-2015 framework for disaster risk reduction that will frame disaster risk policies in the coming decade; and the Sustainable Development Goals that provide a new worldwide normative for development.

S. Kreft, et al

"Global Climate Risk Index 2015," by S. Kreft, D. Eckstein, L. Junghans, C. Kerestan, and U. Hagen, Germanwatch, November 2014.

In Eastern Africa, Climate Change Affects Food Security

International Federation of Red Cross and Red Crescent Societies

The Red Cross and Red Crescent Societies work to bring aid and relief to people in times of need. The following viewpoint explains the environmental upheaval happening in parts of Africa because of climate change and how it could potentially affect the production of food.

As you read, consider the following questions:

1. What diseases have reappeared as a result of climate change?
2. What lakes and rivers have dried up?
3. What percentage of people in eastern Africa rely on agriculture to survive?

Climate change is likely to be aggravating the chronic food shortages in many parts of Eastern Africa. In some countries, 95% of the people depend on agriculture for their livelihood, most of it without irrigation. Erratic rainfall patterns continue to severely disrupt local food production.

"The drought has affected everyone," says Oscar Murengeratwari, a farmer in Burundi. "In former times I could never imagine that

"Climate change makes food security situation worse in Eastern Africa," International Federation of Red Cross and Red Crescent Societies (IFRC), October 18, 2007. Reprinted by Permission.

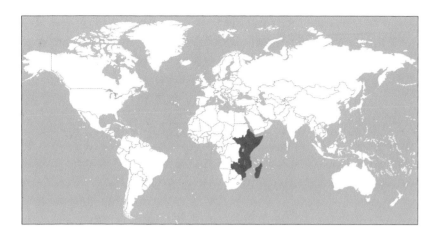

I would have to beg or get food assistance."

New research suggests that the climate change threat is greater in Africa than many parts of the world—on average the continent is 0.5°C warmer than it was a hundred years ago. And the changing weather patterns are already creating new complex emergencies where areas are simultaneously hit by drought and floods, often accompanied by outbreaks of infectious diseases.

Diseases such as cholera and Rift Valley Fever, which were thought to have been eradicated, have now re-appeared. Many communities are living through almost permanent disaster conditions.

"Now it is time to start preparing vulnerable communities for the worst. Climate change is one of the main risks facing humanity today," says Madeleen Helmer, head of the Red Cross/Red Crescent Climate Change Centre in The Hague, Netherlands.

Burundi, where more than half the population live on less than one US dollar a day, has been hit by a series of droughts and floods—for example, drought in 2006 followed by floods in 2007. This year, two million people have been hit by floods and in need of assistance, almost 25% of the population. Crops and livestock were destroyed. Many people, even today, only have one meal a day, others survive on food relief.

"The most visible aspect of climate change is famine—brought on by drought and floods," says Jean Marie Sabushimike, Professor of Geography at the University of Burundi.

Disaster response is an expensive task for the government. According to Nintunga Servilien, head of a government department on Disaster Management in Burundi, almost USD 74 million has been spent in 2007 in the drought-hit province of Kirundo, mostly for food relief and medicines. Disaster preparedness would be a better use of resources. He says: "We have to integrate disaster risk reduction in development programmes now."

There are also worrying signs of lakes and rivers drying up. In Fadis, the eastern part of Ethiopia, the River Boco has completely dried up—partly as a result of a lack of rainfall. The river used to be the main source of irrigation in the area. Yusuf Idris, a local village elder, remembers the fertile soil and orange groves that used to be here. Today his farm produces so little that his children end up having to go to nearby towns to sell their labour and engage in petty trade. Indeed, Yusuf and many others in the area have ended up living on food relief.

Nearby, Lake Haromaya, dried up four years ago. Today, it is a patchwork of small farms. Fatiya Abatish Jacob is a local trader who lived near the lake for 14 years. She laments: "I used to get my drinking water from the lake, now I have to walk 8 km to get it. Also there were many vegetables farmers round here using the water for irrigation and we used to get fish. Now there's no fish round here and vegetables are more expensive."

Adds Ahmed Abdi, who used to be a fisherman on the lake: "I used to catch Nile Perch and other small fish. Now I have no income." The lake also previously supplied water to the nearby town of Harar; the town now suffers from serious water shortages.

It is a similar situation in Rwanda. In Bugesera region, where around 40% of the people are never sure where their next meal is coming from, many farmers have suffered one bad harvest after another due to late or erratic rainfall.

Among them is farmer Mary Jane Nzabamwita. Last year, she estimates, her harvest was down by 50%, this year by 40%. Yet she has five children to feed and to send to school.

"I feel I do not have any freedom, I feel like I am going backwards. The children are not doing so well. When you see a child of 10 years you will think he is only five," says Mary Jane. Her 67-year old mother, who lives with her family, adds: "I have lived here for 21 years and these last years have been the worst."

Not surprisingly, there are high levels of migration in the area as people try and find food and work in other parts of the country or even go to neighbouring countries such as Tanzania.

The Red Cross societies in these countries are beginning to give serious thought to the impact of climate change—particularly since the worst hit are often those already vulnerable. The Red Cross/ Red Crescent has something unique to contribute to the debate and the ongoing work to mitigate the impact of climate change.

Anselme Katyunguruza, the secretary-general of the Burundi Red Cross, is among those who see a clear role for the Red Cross/ Red Crescent in this area. "We need to train our volunteers so that they can integrate the early warning system in other activities," he says. "Our advantage is that volunteers live in every village of the country so we always get 'breaking news' of what's happening at the grassroots level."

And Youcef Ait-Chellouche, the International Federation's Disaster Management Coordinator in West and Central Africa, points out: "Our expertise in disaster management, our close relationship with the community and our work with community-based approaches mean that we are in a good position to adapt to and help communities prepare for changes in disaster patterns due to the climate."

Extreme Weather May Lead to Extreme Hunger

Physicians for Social Responsibility

Physicians for Social Responsibility (PSR) works to create a healthy, just, and peaceful world for both present and future generations. The organization advocates for many issues, including reversing the trajectory toward climate change. In the following viewpoint, it explains the connection between climate change and the potential for widespread famine.

As you read, consider the following questions:

1. What are some specific impacts of climate change?
2. How do changes in glaciers, rivers, and sea levels affect agriculture?
3. How will climate change and extreme weather affect food prices?

Climate change is already threatening the Earth's ability to produce food. These effects are expected to worsen as climate change worsens. Estimates vary, but for every 1.8°F increase in global average surface temperature, we can expect about a 10% decline in yields of the world's major grain crops—corn, soybean, rice and wheat.[1,2] Climate experts predict that global temperature may rise as much as 5.4°F to 9°F if we continue burning fossil fuels at our current rate.[3] This could lead to 30% to 50% declines in crop production.[1] Already, one in seven people, including many living in the U.S., is hungry every day.[4]

Most models only consider the effect of rising temperatures and carbon dioxide (CO_2) levels on crop growth, and thus represent relatively conservative scenarios. Climate change will disrupt food production and distribution in other ways that are hard to quantify and include in prediction models, such as:

- More droughts causing large-scale crop loss

- Increasing frequent, severe, and longer-lasting heat waves killing crops

- Thriving plant pests and diseases destroying crops

- Heavy rains and storms flooding fields, eroding soils and washing away crops

- Melting glaciers and changing river flows reducing water availability for irrigation

- Rising sea levels and storm surges flooding crops and salting soils

- Higher ozone levels damaging plants and reducing crop yields

Specific Climate Change Impacts

Rising Temperatures: The effects of warmer temperatures on crop production will vary by region and crop, but almost all estimates indicate eventual reduced overall crop yields.[1, 5] Higher temperatures decrease rates of photosynthesis, reduce soil moisture, increase water demand and lead to increased survival of plant pests, diseases and weeds—all of which combine to reduce final yields.[1, 5, 6, 7]

Increasing CO_2: In certain plants, like wheat, soybeans and rice, higher CO_2 levels actually increase growth by the "CO_2 fertilization effect".[1, 2, 6] Higher CO_2 levels increase photosynthesis and reduce plant water loss.[1, 5, 6] However most experts agree that the CO_2-related benefits on some crops will be outweighed by other negative effects of climate change as global temperatures continue to rise.[2, 8, 9]

Increasing Temperature Extremes: An increase in the number of days of extreme heat leads to large declines in crop yields, especially when they occur during key stages of plant development such as flowering and grain-filling.[1, 5, 19] Extreme heat damages photosynthetic and reproductive cells, causing decreased growth and sterility, and can decrease grain quality.[5, 6, 10, 11]

Increasing Drought: Climate change will cause more frequent, severe and long-lasting droughts. Many of the largest crop losses in history can be attributed to drought and it is the main cause of year-to-year variations in yields.[5, 10] Eighty percent of agriculture is rain-fed and especially susceptible to drought,[5] but even irrigated agriculture is threatened by drought as stored water supplies are depleted.[10] The area of land producing major crops (corn, rice, soy, wheat, sorghum and barley) affected by drought has risen from 5–10% in the 1960s to 15–25% today.[12]

Heavy Rains, Floods and Tropical Storms: Extreme rainfall events and intensity of tropical storms is increasing.[5] Rainfall intensity could increase by 25% in many agricultural areas.[5] Heavy rainfalls reduce crop productivity by a number of mechanisms. Flooding wipes out vast areas of crops and damages others. In Bangladesh in 2007, cyclone Sidr damaged 1.6 million acres of cropland and over 25% of the rice crop.[13] Heavy rains also cause significant soil erosion reducing long-term productivity. Waterlogged soils reduce plant growth and increase fungal diseases.[5, 6] Farming operations are often delayed when soils are too wet for heavy machinery and flooding can destroy farming supplies, machinery and other infrastructure.[5] Finally, coastal storm surges contribute to soil salinization making widespread areas unfit for planting.[5]

Melting Glaciers and Changing River Flows: Glaciers are a critical water supply for drinking and irrigation but the majority of the world's glaciers are shrinking.[14] Glacier runoff provides water through the year where rainfall is limited, allowing irrigation during dry seasons.[5] Receding glaciers threaten large rivers, such as the Ganges, Indus and Brahmaputra in India, on which over 500 million people depend, to become seasonal—devastating regional agriculture if adaptations are not made.[5, 15]

Sea Level Rise: As sea levels rise, low-lying coastal agriculture in major river deltas and small island nations is especially vulnerable.[5] Rising seas and storm surges will inundate agricultural lands, and salinization of soils and aquifers will threaten agriculture.[5]

Pests and Diseases: Many crop pests, such as aphids and weevils, grow better and live in a wider range of areas in warmer temperatures and higher CO_2 levels.[5] Changes in climate also shift the geographic range and frequency of crop diseases, altering the predictability of outbreaks.[2, 5, 17] Environmental stresses may cause mutations in crop diseases that increase their destructiveness. Heat and water stress reduce crop resistance to pests and diseases.[5]

Weeds: Certain invasive weeds, such as privet and kudzu in the United States, benefit from increasing temperatures and CO_2 levels more than crops.[17] There is evidence that herbicides may lose effectiveness at elevated CO_2 levels.[17] As increasing amounts of herbicide are required to maintain productivity, significant economic, environmental and health costs will result.[17]

Increasing Ozone: Ground-level ozone is a major air pollutant that results from burning fossil fuels.[9] Ozone inhibits photosynthesis and stunts plant growth.[5, 6, 9] Current ozone levels are already suppressing yields of many crops (alfalfa, beans, peanut, potato, rice, soy and wheat) and these effects will worsen as ozone levels continue to rise.[9]

Conclusion

Farmers are resilient and frequently adapt to changes in weather. However, climate change will create conditions outside of human experience, challenging farmers' ability to adapt.[5] While farmers with more wealth and resources are more likely to be able to adapt to a changing climate through investments in new technologies, seed

Climate Change's Humanitarian Impact

Climate change is not just a distant future threat. It is the main driver behind rising humanitarian needs and we are seeing its impact. The number of people affected and the damages inflicted by extreme weather has been unprecedented.

People who are particularly vulnerable include those whose lives are already threatened by abject poverty, HIV/AIDS, environmental degradation, inadequate housing and insecurity. Those living in disaster hot spots—such as flood plains or cyclone tracks—are exposed to repeated climatic shocks that compound their vulnerability. With the threat of extreme weather in the future, the demand for disaster response can only rise, as will the costs.

Tackling climate change needs a global and comprehensive response: curbing greenhouse gases, helping people adapt to changing weather and investing in risk reduction. But for humanitarians, there is one clear-cut challenge: to ensure an effective disaster response.

"Climate Change — Humanitarian Impact," United Nations.

varieties and cropping patterns, poorer subsistence farmers will be less likely to adapt and are thus more vulnerable.[1, 2, 6] Regardless of wealth, complete adaptation is not possible.

Increasing extreme weather events has the potential to devastate infrastructure of the entire food system.[10] Storms and flooding can destroy food processing, packaging and storage facilities and disrupt transportation infrastructure such as roads, bridges, railways, airports and shipping routes preventing available food from getting to where it is needed.[10, 17]

Though this fact sheet focuses on agricultural crops, they are only one part of the food supply. The changing climate also affects animal production. Decreasing supply and increasing prices of feed grains will increase the price of meat.[1, 9] Temperature extremes will increase animal deaths and the cost of cooling animal facilities.[1, 9] Rising temperatures and changing rainfall patterns will alter the distribution of animal diseases such as anthrax and blackleg, potentially reducing production.[9] The overall impact on fisheries is uncertain, however a 40% catch decline is expected in the tropics as commercial species move north out of warming waters.[1]

Food prices will rise as climate change reduces the amount of food available. And people get angry, even violent, when food becomes more expensive. In 2008, world wheat, rice, corn and soybean prices tripled.[18] Food riots erupted across Egypt, Yemen, Morocco, Cameroon, Senegal, Ethiopia, Haiti, Indonesia, Mexico, and the Philippines.[18] Social order unraveled as armed Thai villagers guarded their rice fields against rice rustlers; grain trucks were hijacked in Sudanese refugee camps; Pakistani troops had to guard grain elevators and wheat trucks.[18] There is concern about increased conflict and violence as food supplies constrict.

Already one billion people in the world go hungry every day—that's one in every seven people.[18] Every year one third of child deaths are caused in part by under-nutrition.[19] World population continues to grow and is expected to reach 9 billion by 2050.[20] To feed this many people and their rising demand for animal products, overall food production must rise by 70% from 2005–07 levels.[20] But a 5°F to 9°F rise in global average temperature could reduce grain yields by 30% to 50%, and global food supplies even more. The combination of decreasing food production in the face of increasing food demand would likely lead to widespread social unrest and hunger—even catastrophic global famine.

This is the future that awaits us if we fail to act. But we can rewrite the future from this grim view IF we work to create many solutions, from efficiencies to new renewable energy, to reduce greenhouse gas emissions by 80% by 2050. To find out how you can get involved in making a better future, visit www.psr.org to discover actions going on in your area.

Endnotes

1. Committee on Stabilization Targets for Atmospheric Greenhouse Gas Concentrations, Board of Atmospheric Sciences and Climate, Division of Earth and Life Studies, National Research Council. Climate stabilization targets: Emissions, concentrations, and impacts over decades to millennia. National Academies of Sciences. 2011.

2. Henson R. Warming world: Impacts by a degree. National Academies of Sciences. 2011.

3. National Research Council (NRC). Advancing the science of climate change. National Academies of Sciences. 2010.

4. Food and Agriculture Organization of the United Nations. The State of Food Insecurity in the World. 2012.

5. Gornall J, Betts R, Burke E, et al. Implications of climate change for agricultural productivity in the early twenty-first century. *Philos Trans R Soc Lond B Biol Sci.* 2010;365(1554):2973–2989.

6. Lobell DB, Gourdji SM. The influence of climate change on global crop productivity. *Plant Physiol.* 2012;160(4):1686–1697.

7. Ziska LH, Blumenthal DM, Runion GB, Hunt ER, Diaz-Soltero H. Invasive species and climate change: An agronomic perspective. *Clim Change.* 2011;105:13–42.

8. Long SP, Ainsworth EA, Leakey AD, Morgan PB. Global food insecurity. treatment of major food crops with elevated carbon dioxide or ozone under large-scale fully open-air conditions suggests recent models may have overestimated future yields. *Philos Trans R Soc Lond B Biol Sci.* 2005;360(1463):2011–2020.

9. United States Department of Agriculture (USDA). Climate change and agriculture in the United States: Effects and adaptation. 2013; USDA Technical Bulletin 1935:1–186.

10. Handmer J, Honda Y, Kundzewicz ZW, et al. Changes in impacts of climate extremes: Human systems and ecosystems. In: Managing the risks of extreme events and disasters to advance climate change adaptation. A special report of working groups I and II of the intergovernmental panel on climate change (IPCC). 2012: 231–290.

11. Teixeira EI, Fischer G, van Velthuizen H, Walter C, Ewert F. Global hotspots of heat stress on agricultural crops due to climate change. *Agric For Meteorol.* 2013;170(15):206–215.

12. Li YP, Ye W, Wang M, Yan XD. Climate change and drought: A risk assessment of crop yield impacts. *Clim Res.* 2009;39:31–46.

13. United Nations. Cyclone Sidr United Nations rapid initial assessment report. 2007. http://ochaonline.un.org/News/NaturalDisasters/Bangladesh/ tabid/2707/Default.aspx

14. Zemp M, et.al. Global glacier changes: Facts and figures. UNEP world glacier monitoring service. 2008.

15. Kehrwald NM, Thompson LG, Yao TD, et al. Mass loss on Himalayan glacier endangers water resources. *Geophys Res Lett.* 2008;35(L22503).

16. Gregory PJ, Johnson SN, Newton AC, Ingram JS. Integrating pests and pathogens into the climate change/food security debate. *J Exp Bot.* 2009; 60:2827–2838.

17. Hatfield J, Takle G, Grotjahn R, et al. Chapter 6: Agriculture. In Draft of National climate assessment development. 2013;11 Jan:227– 261. http://ncadac.globalchange.gov/download/NCAJan11-2013- publicreviewdraft-chap6-agriculture.pdf

18. Brown L. *World on the edge: How to prevent environmental and economic collapse.* First ed. New York, NY: W.W. Norton & Company, Inc.; 2011:240.

19. United Nations Inter-Agency Group for Child Mortality Estimation. Levels and trends in child mortality. Report 2011. 2011:1–19.

20. Food and Agricultural Organization (FAO), Office of the Director, Agricultural Development Economics Division Economic and Social Development Department. High level expert forum—How to feed the world 2050. 2009.

Periodical and Internet Sources Bibliography

The following articles have been selected to supplement the diverse views presented in this chapter.

Mona Ahmadiani and Susana Ferreira, "Well-being Effects of Extreme Weather Events in the US," Agricultural & Applied Economics Association Annual Meeting, 2016. http:// ageconsearch.umn.edu/bitstream/236259/2/Ahmadiani_ Ferreira_AAEA2016.pdf.

Canadian Broadcasting Corporation News, "Facing the Change: Toronto Grapples with the Effects of Extreme Weather," CBC News, September 17, 2016. http://www.cbc.ca/news/canada /toronto/day-6-climate-change-toronto-1.3766155.

Terra Daily, "Effects of Extreme Weather Impacting Society More," Terra Daily, October 8, 2000. http://www.spacedaily.com/news /weather-00l.html.

Janet Davison, "Is Extreme Weather the New Normal?" CBC News, August 8, 2013. http://www.cbc.ca/news/canada/is-extreme -weather-the-new-normal-1.1321493.

J. Ewald, et al., "Effects of Extreme Weather, Climate and Pesticides on Farmland Invertebrates," *Science for Environmental Policy*, October 8, 2015.

Malte Jahn, "Economics of Extreme Weather Events: Terminology and Regional Impact Models," *Journal of Weather and Climate Extremes*, December 2015.

Raymond P. Motha, "The Impact of Extreme Weather Events on Agriculture in the United States," Publications from USDA-ARS / UNL Faculty, Paper 1311. http://digitalcommons.unl.edu/cgi /viewcontent.cgi?article=2316&context=usdaarsfacpub.

Kenneth Rogoff, "What Impact Does Extreme Weather Have on the Global Economy?" World Economic Forum, January 12, 2016. https://www.weforum.org/agenda/2016/01/what-impact-does -extreme-weather-have-on-the-global-economy.

State of Washington Department of Ecology, "More Extreme Weather Events." http://www.ecy.wa.gov/climatechange/extremeweather_ more.htm.

University of East Anglia (UK), "Extreme Weather Effects May Explain Recent Butterfly Decline," Phys.org, October 31, 2016. https://phys.org/news/2016-10-extreme-weather-effects -butterfly-decline.html.

Amelia Xu, "5 Ways the Weather Affects the Economy," Smart Asset, February 3, 2017. https://smartasset.com/mortgage/5-ways-the -weather-affects-the-economy.

GLOBALVIEWPOINTS

CHAPTER 3

Extreme Weather and Global Warming

Global Warming Is Man-made, Not Myth

Donald R. Prothero

The Skeptics Society is a nonprofit organization devoted to promoting scientific skepticism and resisting the spread of pseudoscience, superstition, and irrational beliefs. In the following viewpoint, Donald R. Prothero, writing for the society, presents evidence that points to global warming as a real phenomenon that has been caused by human activity.

As you read, consider the following questions:

1. What lines of evidence does the author present to prove global warming exists?
2. What is one argument used to deny climate change?
3. What are some of the reasons why people deny climate change?

On January 27, 2012, the *Wall Street Journal* ran an Opinion Editorial written by 16 people who deny the evidence of human-induced climate change. Most of the authors of the editorial were not climate scientists; one of two actual climate scientists of the group, Richard Lindzen, is a notorious global warming denier who also denies that smoking causes cancer. Predictably, the Rupert Murdoch-owned *Journal* refused to run a statement by 255 members of the National Academy of Sciences, although

"How We Know Global Warming Is Real and Human Caused," by Donald R. Prothero, The Skeptics Society, January 27, 2012. Reprinted by permission.

a "Letter to the Editor" by 38 of the world's leading climate scientists[1] did manage to get published there. The letter pointed out the numerous lies, mistakes, and fallacies in the editorial, along with a scathing rebuke by climate scientist Kevin Trenberth, whose remarks were quoted out of context to make them seem the opposite of what he actually said. As the Trenberth et al. letter pointed out, the 16 authors of the editorial were so far out of their depth in discussing the topic that they were the "climate-science equivalent of dentists practicing cardiology." And as if to answer the editorial, the earth sent a resounding message in reply. On Feb. 2, 2012, an 18-mile crack appeared in Pine Island Glacier in Antarctica, a prelude to the calving off an iceberg 350 square miles in area, one of the largest icebergs ever seen.[2]

Converging Lines of Evidence

How do we know that global warming is real and primarily human caused? There are numerous lines of evidence that converge to this conclusion.

1. **Carbon Dioxide Increase**. Carbon dioxide in our atmosphere has increased at an unprecedented rate in the past 200 years. Not one data set collected over a long enough span of time shows otherwise. Mann et al. (1999) compiled the past 900 years' worth of temperature data from tree rings, ice cores, corals, and direct measurements of the past few centuries, and the sudden increase of temperature of the past century stands out like a sore thumb. This famous graph is now known as the "hockey stick" because it is long and straight through most of its length, then bends sharply upward at the end like the blade of a hockey stick. Other graphs show that climate was very stable within a narrow range of variation through the past 1000, 2000, or even 10,000 years since the end of the last Ice Age. There were minor warming events during the Climatic Optimum about 7000 years ago, the Medieval Warm Period, and the slight cooling

of the Little Ice Age from the 1700s and 1800s. But the magnitude and rapidity of the warming represented by the last 200 years is simply unmatched in all of human history. More revealing, the timing of this warming coincides with the Industrial Revolution, when humans first began massive deforestation and released carbon dioxide by burning coal, gas, and oil.

2. **Melting Polar Ice Caps**. The polar icecaps are thinning and breaking up at an alarming rate. In 2000, my former graduate advisor Malcolm McKenna was one of the first humans to fly over the North Pole in summer time and see no ice, just open water. The Arctic ice cap has been frozen solid for at least the past 3 million years and maybe longer,[3] but now the entire ice sheet is breaking up so fast that by 2030 (and possibly sooner) less than half of the Arctic will be ice covered in the summer.[4] As one can see from watching the news, this is an ecological disaster for everything that lives up there, from the polar bears to the seals and walruses to the animals they feed upon, to the 4 million people whose world is melting beneath their feet. The Antarctic is thawing even faster. In February–March 2002, the Larsen B ice shelf—over 3000 square km (the size of Rhode Island) and 220 m (700 feet) thick—broke up in just a few months, a story typical of nearly all the ice shelves in Antarctica. The Larsen B shelf had survived all the previous ice ages and interglacial warming episodes for the past 3 million years, and even the warmest periods of the last 10,000 years—yet it and nearly all the other thick ice sheets on the Arctic, Greenland, and Antarctic are vanishing at a rate never before seen in geologic history.

3. **Melting Glaciers**. Glaciers are all retreating at the highest rates ever documented. Many of those glaciers, especially in the Himalayas, Andes, Alps, and Sierras, provide most of the freshwater that the populations below the mountains depend upon—yet this fresh water supply

is vanishing. Just think about the percentage of world's population in southern Asia (especially India) that depend on Himalayan snowmelt for their fresh water. The implications are staggering. The permafrost that once remained solidly frozen even in the summer has now thawed, damaging the Inuit villages on the Arctic coast and threatening all our pipelines to the North Slope of Alaska. This is catastrophic not only for life on the permafrost, but as it thaws, the permafrost releases huge amounts of greenhouse gases and is one of the major contributors to global warming. Not only is the ice vanishing, but we have seen record heat waves over and over again, killing thousands of people, as each year joins the list of the hottest years on record. (2010 just topped that list as the hottest year, surpassing the previous record in 2009, and we shall know about 2011 soon enough). Natural animal and plant populations are being devastated all over the globe as their environment changes.[5] Many animals respond by moving their ranges to formerly cold climates, so now places that once did not have to worry about disease-bearing mosquitoes are infested as the climate warms and allows them to breed further north.

4. **Sea Level Rise**. All that melted ice eventually ends up in the ocean, causing sea level to rise, as it has many times in the geologic past. At present, sea level is rising about 3–4 mm per year, more than ten times the rate of 0.1–0.2 mm/year that has occurred over the past 3000 years. Geological data show that sea level was virtually unchanged over the past 10,000 years since the present interglacial began. A few millimeters here or there doesn't impress people, until you consider that the rate is accelerating and that most scientists predict sea level will rise 80–130 cm in just the next century. A sea level rise of 1.3 m (almost 4 feet) would drown many of the world's low-elevation cities, such as Venice and New

Orleans, and low-lying countries such as the Netherlands or Bangladesh. A number of tiny island nations such as Vanuatu and the Maldives, which barely poke out above the ocean now, are already vanishing beneath the waves. Eventually their entire population will have to move someplace else.[6] Even a small sea level rise might not drown all these areas, but they are much more vulnerable to the large waves of a storm surge (as happened with Hurricane Katrina), which could do much more damage than sea level rise alone. If sea level rose by 6 m (20 feet), most of the world's coastal plains and low-lying areas (such as the Louisiana bayous, Florida, and most of the world's river deltas) would be drowned.

Most of the world's population lives in coastal cities such as New York, Boston, Philadelphia, Baltimore, Washington, D.C., Miami, Shanghai, and London. All of those cities would be partially or completely under water with such a sea level rise. If all the glacial ice caps melted completely (as they have several times before during past greenhouse episodes in the geologic past), sea level would rise by 65 m (215 feet)! The entire Mississippi Valley would flood, so you could dock your boat in Cairo, Illinois. Such a sea level rise would drown nearly every coastal region under hundreds of feet of water, and inundate New York City, London and Paris. All that would remain would be the tall landmarks, such as the Empire State Building, Big Ben, and the Eiffel Tower. You could tie your boats to these pinnacles, but the rest of these drowned cities would be deep under water.

Climate Deniers' Arguments and Scientists' Rebuttals

Despite the overwhelming evidence there are many people who remain skeptical. One reason is that they have been fed lies, distortions, and misstatements by the global warming denialists who want to cloud or confuse the issue. Let's examine some of these claims in detail:

- **"It's just natural climatic variability."** *No, it is not.* Geologists and paleoclimatologists know a lot about past greenhouse worlds, and the icehouse planet that has existed for the past 33 million years. We have a good understanding of how and why the Antarctic ice sheet first appeared at that time, and how the Arctic froze over about 3.5 million years ago, beginning the 24 glacial and interglacial episodes of the "Ice Ages" that have occurred since then. We know how variations in the earth's orbit (the Milankovitch cycles) controls the amount of solar radiation the earth receives, triggering the shifts between glacial and interglacial periods. Our current warm interglacial has already lasted 10,000 years, the duration of most previous interglacials, so if it were not for global warming, we would be headed into the next glacial in the next 1000 years or so. Instead, our pumping greenhouse gases into our atmosphere after they were long trapped in the earth's crust has pushed the planet into a "super-interglacial," already warmer than any previous warming period. We can see the "big picture" of climate variability most clearly in the EPICA (European Project for Ice Coring in Antarctica) cores from Antarctica which show the details of the last 650,000 years of glacial-interglacial cycles. *At no time during any previous interglacial did the carbon dioxide levels exceed 300 ppm, even at their very warmest.* Our atmospheric carbon dioxide levels are already close to 400 ppm today. The atmosphere is headed to 600 ppm within a few decades, even if we stopped releasing greenhouse gases immediately. This is decidedly *not* within the normal range of "climatic variability," but clearly unprecedented in human history. Anyone who says this is "normal variability" has never seen the huge amount of paleoclimatic data that show otherwise.

- "It's just another warming episode, like the Mediaeval Warm Period, or the Holocene Climatic Optimum" or the end of the Little Ice Age." *Untrue.* There were numerous small fluctuations of warming and cooling over the last 10,000 years of the Holocene. But in the case of the Mediaeval Warm Period (about 950–1250 A.D.), the temperatures increased by only 1°C, much less than we have seen in the current episode of global warming. This episode was also only a local warming in the North Atlantic and northern Europe. Global temperatures over this interval did not warm at all, and actually cooled by more than 1°C. Likewise, the warmest period of the last 10,000 years was the Holocene Climatic Optimum (5000–9000 B.C.) when warmer and wetter conditions in Eurasia caused the rise of the first great civilizations in Egypt, Mesopotamia, the Indus Valley, and China. This was largely a Northern Hemisphere-Eurasian phenomenon, with 2–3°C warming in the Arctic and northern Europe. But there was almost no warming in the tropics, and cooling or no change in the Southern Hemisphere.[7] To the Eurocentric world, these warming events seemed important, but on a global scale the effect is negligible. In addition, neither of these warming episodes is related to increasing greenhouse gases. The Holocene Climatic Optimum, in fact, is predicted by the Milankovitch cycles, since at that time the axial tilt of the earth was 24°, its steepest value, meaning the Northern Hemisphere got more solar radiation than normal—but the Southern Hemisphere less, so the two balanced. By contrast, not only is the warming observed in the last 200 years much greater than during these previous episodes, but it is also *global and bipolar*, so it is not a purely local effect. The warming that ended the Little Ice Age (from the mid-1700s to the late 1800s) was due to increased solar radiation prior to 1940. Since 1940, however, the amount of solar radiation has been dropping, so the only candidate for the post-1940 warming has to be carbon dioxide.[8]

- **"It's just the sun, or cosmic rays, or volcanic activity or methane."** *Nope, sorry.* The amount of heat that the sun provides has been decreasing since 1940,[9] just the opposite of the denialists' claims. There is no evidence of increase in cosmic radiation during the past century.[10] Nor is there any clear evidence that large-scale volcanic events (such as the 1815 eruption of Tambora in Indonesia, which changed global climate for about a year) have any long-term effect that would explain 200 years of warming and carbon dioxide increase. Volcanoes erupt only 0.3 billion tonnes of carbon dioxide each year, but humans emit over 29 billion tonnes a year,[11] roughly 100 times as much. Clearly, we have a bigger effect. Methane is a more powerful greenhouse gas, but there is 200 times more carbon dioxide than methane, so carbon dioxide is still the most important agent.[12] Every other alternative has been looked at, but the only clear-cut relationship is between human-caused carbon dioxide increase and global warming.

- **"The climate records since 1995 (or 1998) show cooling."** *That's a deliberate deception.* People who throw this argument out are cherry-picking the data.[13] Over the short term, there was a slight cooling trend from 1998–2000 because 1998 was a record-breaking El Niño year, so the next few years look cooler by comparison. But since 2002, the overall long-term trend of warming is unequivocal. This statement is a clear-cut case of using out-of-context data in an attempt to deny reality. All of the 16 hottest years ever recorded on a global scale have occurred in the last 20 years. They are (in order of hottest first): 2010, 2009, 1998, 2005, 2003, 2002, 2004, 2006, 2007, 2001, 1997, 2008, 1995, 1999, 1990, and 2000.[14] In other words, every year since 2000 has been in the Top Ten hottest years list, and the rest of the list includes 1995, 1997, 1998, 1999, and 2000. Only 1996 failed to make the list (because of the short-term cooling mentioned already).

- **"We had record snows in the winters of 2009–2010, and in 2010–2011."** *So what?* This is nothing more than the difference between *weather* (short-term seasonal changes) and *climate* (the long-term average of weather over decades and centuries and longer). Our local weather tells us nothing about another continent, or the global average; it is only a local effect, determined by short-term atmospheric and oceanographic conditions.[15] In fact, warmer global temperatures mean *more moisture* in the atmosphere, which increases the intensity of normal winter snowstorms. In this particular case, the climate denialists forget that the early winter of November–December 2009 was actually very mild and warm, and then only later in January and February did it get cold and snow heavily. That warm spell in early winter helped bring *more moisture* into the system, so that when cold weather occurred, the snows were worse. In addition, the snows were unusually heavy only in North America; the rest of the world had different weather, and the global climate was warmer than average. And the summer of 2010 was the hottest on record, breaking the previous record set in 2009.

- **"Carbon dioxide is good for plants, so the world will be better off."** *Who do they think they're kidding?* The people who promote this idea clearly don't know much global geochemistry, or are trying to cynically take advantage of the fact that most people are ignorant of science. The Competitive Enterprise Institute (funded by oil and coal companies and conservative foundations[16]) has run a series of shockingly stupid ads concluding with the tag line "Carbon dioxide: they call it pollution, we call it life." Anyone who knows the basic science of earth's atmosphere can spot the deceptions in this ad.[17] Sure, plants take in carbon dioxide that animals exhale, as they have for millions of years. But the whole point of the global warming evidence (as shown from ice cores) is that the delicate natural balance of carbon dioxide has been thrown out of whack by our production of too much of it, way in excess of what plants or the oceans can handle. As a consequence, the oceans are warming[18] and absorbing excess carbon dioxide making them more acidic.

Already we are seeing a shocking decline in coral reefs ("bleaching") and extinctions in many marine ecosystems that can't handle too much of a good thing. Meanwhile, humans are busy cutting down huge areas of temperate and tropical forests, which not only means there are fewer plants to absorb the gas, but the slash and burn practices are releasing more carbon dioxide than plants can keep up with. There is much debate as to whether increased carbon dioxide might help agriculture in some parts of the world, but that has to be measured against the fact that other traditional "breadbasket" regions (such as the American Great Plains) are expected to get too hot to be as productive as they are today. The latest research[19] actually shows that increased carbon dioxide inhibits the absorption of nitrogen into plants, so plants (at least those that we depend upon today) are *not* going to flourish in a greenhouse world. Anyone who tells you otherwise is ignorant of basic atmospheric science.

- **"I agree that climate is changing, but I'm skeptical that humans are the main cause, so we shouldn't do anything."** *This is just fence sitting.* A lot of reasonable skeptics deplore the "climate denialism" of the right wing, but still want to be skeptical about the cause. If they want proof, they can examine the huge array of data that directly points to humans causing global warming.[20] We can directly measure the amount of carbon dioxide humans are producing, and it tracks exactly with the amount of increase in atmospheric carbon dioxide. Through carbon isotope analysis, we can show that this carbon dioxide in the atmosphere is coming directly from our burning of fossil fuels, not from natural sources. We can also measure oxygen levels that drop as we produce more carbon that then combines with oxygen to produce carbon dioxide. We have satellites in space that are measuring the heat released from the planet and can actually *see* the atmosphere get warmer. The most crucial proof emerged only in the past few years: climate models of the greenhouse effect predict that there should be cooling in the stratosphere (the upper layer of the atmosphere above 10 km (6 miles) in elevation), but warming in the troposphere (the bottom layer of the atmosphere below 10 km (6 miles)), and that's exactly what our space probes have measured. Finally, we can rule out any other culprits: solar heat is decreasing since 1940, not increasing, and there are no measurable increases in cosmic radiation, methane, volcanic gases, or any other potential cause. Face it—it's our problem.

Why Do People Deny Climate Change?

[…]

The right-wing institutes and the energy lobby beat the bushes to find scientists—*any* scientists—who might disagree with the scientific consensus. As investigative journalists and scientists have documented over and over again,[26] the denialist conspiracy essentially paid for the testimony of anyone who could be useful to them. The day that the 2007 IPCC report was released (Feb. 2, 2007), the British newspaper *The Guardian* reported that the conservative American Enterprise Institute (funded largely by oil companies and conservative think tanks) had offered $10,000 plus travel expenses to scientists who would write negatively about the IPCC report.[27]

We are accustomed to the hired-gun "experts" paid by lawyers to muddy up the evidence in the case they are fighting, but this is extraordinary—buying scientists outright to act as shills for organizations trying to deny scientific reality. With this kind of money, however, you can always find a fringe scientist or crank or someone with no relevant credentials who will do what they're paid to do.

The NCSE satirized this tactic of composing phony "lists of scientists" with their "Project Steve."[28] They showed that there were more scientists named "Steve" than their entire list of "scientists who dispute evolution." It may generate lots of PR and a smokescreen to confuse the public, but it doesn't change the fact that *scientists who actually do research in climate change are unanimous in their insistence that anthropogenic global warming is a real threat.* Most scientists I know and respect work very hard for little pay, yet they still cannot be paid to endorse some scientific idea they know to be false.

The climate deniers have a lot of other things in common with creationists and other anti-science movements. They too like to quote someone out of context ("quote mining"), finding a short phrase in the work of legitimate scientists that seems to support their position. But when you read the full quote in context, it is obvious that they have used the quote inappropriately. The original author meant something that does not support their goals. The "Climategate scandal" is a classic case of this. It started with a few stolen emails from the Climate Research Unit of the University of East Anglia. If you read the complete text of the actual emails[29] and comprehend the scientific shorthand of climate scientists who are talking casually to each other, it is clear that there was no great "conspiracy" or that they were faking data. All six subsequent investigations have cleared Philip Jones and the other scientists of the University of East Anglia of any wrongdoing or conspiracy.[30]

Even *if* there had been some conspiracy on the part of these few scientists, there is no reason to believe that the entire climate science community is secretly working together to generate false information and mislead the public. If there's one thing that is clear about science, it's about competition and criticism, not conspiracy and collusion. Most labs are competing with each other, not conspiring together. If one lab publishes a result that is not clearly defensible, other labs will quickly correct it. As James Lawrence Powell wrote[31]:

> Scientists….show no evidence of being more interested in politics or ideology than the average American. Does it make sense to believe that tens of thousands of scientists would be so deeply and secretly committed to bringing down capitalism and

the American way of life that they would spend years beyond their undergraduate degrees working to receive master's and Ph.D. degrees, then go to work in a government laboratory or university, plying the deep oceans, forbidding deserts, icy poles, and torrid jungles, all for far less money than they could have made in industry, all the while biding their time like a Russian sleeper agent in an old spy novel? Scientists tend to be independent and resist authority. That is why you are apt to find them in the laboratory or in the field, as far as possible from the prying eyes of a supervisor. Anyone who believes he could organize thousands of scientists into a conspiracy has never attended a single faculty meeting.

There are many more traits that the climate deniers share with the creationists and Holocaust deniers and others who distort the truth. They pick on small disagreements between different labs as if scientists can't get their story straight, when in reality there is always a fair amount of give and take between competing labs as they try to get the answer right before the other lab can do so. The key point here is that when *all* these competing labs around the world have reached a consensus and get the same answer, there is no longer any reason to doubt their common conclusion. The anti-scientists of climate denialism will also point to small errors by individuals in an effort to argue that the entire enterprise cannot be trusted. It is true that scientists are human, and do make mistakes, but the great power of the scientific method is that *peer review weeds these out*, so that when scientists speak with consensus, there is no doubt that their data are checked carefully.

Finally, a powerful line of evidence that this is a purely political controversy, rather than a scientific debate, is that the membership lists of the creationists and the climate deniers are highly overlapping. Both anti-scientific dogmas are fed to their overlapping audiences through right-wing media such as Fox News, Glenn Beck, and Rush Limbaugh. Just take a look at the "intelligent-design" creationism website for the Discovery Institute. Most of the daily news items lately have nothing to do with creationism at all, but are focused on climate denial and other right-wing causes.[32]

If the data about global climate change are indeed valid and robust, any qualified scientist should be able to look at them and see if the prevailing scientific interpretation holds up. Indeed, such a test took place. Starting in 2010, a group led by U.C. Berkeley physicist Richard Muller re-examined all the temperature data from the NOAA, East Anglia Hadley Climate Research Unit, and the Goddard Institute of Space Science sources. Even though Muller started out as a skeptic of the temperature data, and was funded by the Koch brothers and other oil company sources, he carefully checked and re-checked the research himself. When the GOP leaders called him to testify before the House Science and Technology Committee in spring 2011, they were expecting him to discredit the temperature data. Instead, Muller shocked his GOP sponsors by demonstrating his scientific integrity and telling the truth: the temperature increase is real, and the scientists who have demonstrated that the climate is changing are right. In the fall of 2011, his study was published, and the conclusions were clear: global warming is real, even to a right-wing skeptical scientist. Unlike the hired-gun scientists who play political games, Muller did what a true scientist should do: if the data go against your biases and preconceptions, then do the right thing and admit it— even if you've been paid by sponsors who want to discredit global warming. Muller is a shining example of a scientist whose integrity and honesty came first, and did not sell out to the highest bidder.[33]

Science and Anti-Science

The conclusion is clear: there's science, and then there's the anti-science of the global warming denial. As we have seen, there is a nearly unanimous consensus among climate scientists that anthropogenic global warming is real and that we must do something about it. Yet the smokescreen, bluster and lies of the deniers has created enough doubt that only half of the American public is convinced the problem requires action. Ironically, the U.S. is almost alone in their denial of this scientific reality. International polls taken of 33,000 people in 33 nations in 2006 and 2007 show that 90% of their citizens regard climate change as a serious problem[34] and 80% realize that humans are the cause of it.[35] Just as in the case of creationism, the U.S. is out of step with much of the rest of the world in accepting scientific reality.

It is not just the liberals and environmentalists who are taking climate change seriously. Historically conservative institutions (big corporations such as General Electric and many others such as insurance companies and the military) are already planning on how to deal with global warming. Many of my friends high in the oil companies tell me of the efforts by those companies to get into other forms of energy, because they know that oil will be running out soon and that the effects of burning oil will make their business less popular. BP officially stands for "British Petroleum," but in one of their ad campaigns about 5 years ago, it stood for "Beyond Petroleum."[36] Although they still spend relatively little of their total budgets on alternative forms of energy, the oil companies still can see the handwriting on the wall about the eventual exhaustion of oil—and they are acting like any company that wants to survive by getting into a new business when the old one is dying.

The Pentagon (normally not a left-wing institution) is also making contingency plans for how to fight wars in an era of global climate change, and what kinds of strategic threats might occur when climate change alters the kinds of enemies we might be fighting, and water becomes a scarce commodity. The *New York Times* reported[37] that in December 2008, the National Defense University outlined plans for military strategy in a greenhouse world. To the Pentagon, the big issue is global chaos and the potential of even nuclear conflict. The world must "prepare for the inevitable effects of abrupt climate change—which will likely come [the only question is when] regardless of human activity."

Insurance companies have no political axe to grind. If anything, they tend to be on the conservative side. They are simply in the business of assessing risk in a realistic fashion so they can accurately gauge their future insurance policies and what to charge for them. Yet they are all investing heavily in research on the disasters and risks posed by climatic change. In 2005, a study commissioned by the re-insurer Swiss Re said, "Climate change will significantly affect the health of humans and ecosystems and these impacts will have economic consequences."[38]

Some people may still try to deny scientific reality, but big businesses like oil and insurance, and conservative institutions like the military, cannot afford to be blinded or deluded by ideology. They must plan for the real world that we will be seeing in the next few decades. They do not want to be caught unprepared and harmed by global climatic change when it threatens their survival. Neither can we as a society.

Footnotes

1. thinkprogress.org/green/2012/02/01/416078/climate-scientists-rebuke-rupert-murdoch-wsj-denier-op-ed-like-dentists-practicing-cardiology/
2. news.yahoo.com/18-mile-crack-seen-nasa-antarctic-glacier-205345573–abc-news.html
3. www.homepage.montana.edu/~geol445/hyperglac/time1/time.htm
4. Arctic summers ice-free "by 2013." bbc.co.uk. 2007-12-12.
5. Barnosky, A.D. 2009. *Heatstroke: Nature in an Age of Global Warming*. Island Press, Washington, DC.
6. www.ens-newswire.com/ens/dec2005/2005-12-06-02.asp
7. Masson, V., Vimeux, F., Jouzel, J., Morgan, V., Delmotte, M., Ciais,P., Hammer, C., Johnsen, S., Lipenkov, V.Y., Mosley-Thompson, E.,Petit, J.-R., Steig, E.J., Stievenard,M., Vaikmae, R. (2000). "Holocene climate variability in Antarctica based on 11 ice-core isotopic records." *Quaternary Research* 54: 348–358. D.S. Kaufman, T.A. Ager, N.J. Anderson, P.M. Anderson, J.T. Andrews, P.J. Bartlein, L.B. Brubaker, L.L. Coats, L.C. Cwynar, M.L. Duvall, A.S. Dyke, M.E. Edwards, W.R. Eisner, K. Gajewski, A. Geirsdottir, F.S. Hu, A.E. Jennings, M.R. Kaplan, M.W. Kerwin, A.V. Lozhkin, G.M. MacDonald, G.H. Miller, C.J. Mock, W.W. Oswald, B.L. Otto-Bliesner, D.F. Porinchu, K. Ruhland, J.P. Smol, E.J. Steig, B.B. Wolfe (2004). "Holocene thermal maximum in the western Arctic (0–180 W)." *Quaternary Science Reviews* 23: 529–560.
8. www.skepticalscience.com/coming-out-of-little-ice-age.htm
9. www.skepticalscience.com/solar-activity-sunspots-global-warming.htm
10. www.skepticalscience.com/cosmic-rays-and-global-warming.htm
11. www.skepticalscience.com/volcanoes-and-global-warming.htm
12. www.skepticalscience.com/methane-and-global-warming.htm
13. www.skepticalscience.com/global-warming-stopped-in-1998.htm
14. www.nicholas.duke.edu/thegreengrok/2008temps
15. www.skepticalscience.com/global-warming-cold-weather.htm
16. www.exxonsecrets.org/html/orgfactsheet.php
17. www.skepticalscience.com/co2-pollutant.htm
18. www.skepticalscience.com/ocean-and-global-warming.htm
19. Bloom, A.J., Burger, M., Asensio, J.S.R., and Cousins, A.B. 2010. Carbon dioxide enrichment inhibits nitrate assimilation in wheat and *Arabidopsis*. Science 328: 899–903.
20. www.skepticalscience.com/its-not-us.htm

21. www.gallup.com/poll/126560/americans-global-warming-concerns-continue-drop.aspx
22. Oreskes, N. 2004. Beyond the Ivory Tower: The scientific consensus on climatic change. *Science* 306: 1686.
23. Doran, P., and M. Kendall Zimmerman. 2009. Examining the scientific consensus on climatic change. EOS 90 (3): 22.
24. Anderegg, W.R.L., Prall, J.W., Harold, J., and Schneider, S.H. 2010. Expert credibility on climate change. *Proceedings of the National Academy of Sciences* (USA) 107:12107–12109.
25. lightbucket.wordpress.com/2008/04/07/doubt-is-our-product-pr-versus-science/
26. McCright, A. M., Dunlap, R. E. 2003. Defeating Kyoto: The Conservative Movement's Impact on U.S. Climate Change Policy. *Social Problems* 50 (3): 348–373; Curry, J.A., Webster, P.J., and Holland, G.J. 2006. Mixing Politics and Science in Testing the Hypothesis That Greenhouse Warming Is Causing a Global Increase in Hurricane Intensity. *Bulletin of the American Meteorological Society* 87 (8): 1025–1037; Williams, N. 2005. Heavyweight attack on climate-change denial, *Current Biology* 15 (4): R109–R110; Mooney, C. 2006. *The Republican War on Science*. Basic Books, New York; Mooney, C. 2007. *Storm World: Hurricanes, Politics, and the Battle over Global Warming*. Harcourt, New York.Hoggan, J. 2009. *Climate Cover-Up: the Crusade to Deny Global Warming*. Greystone, Vancouver, B.C.; Oreskes, N., and Conway, E.M. 2010. *Merchants of Doubt: How a handful of scientists obscured the truth on the issues from tobacco smoke to global warming*. Bloomsbury Press, New York.
27. Ian Sample, "Scientists offered cash to dispute climate study," *The Guardian*, 2 Feb. 2007.
28. ncse.com/taking-action/project-steve
29. www.realclimate.org/index.php/archives/2009/11/the-cru-hack/
30. www.washingtonpost.com/wp-dyn/content/article/2010/04/14/AR2010041404001.html
31. Powell, J.L. 2011. *The Inquisition of Climate Science*, p. 187
32. sensuouscurmudgeon.wordpress.com/2010/03/19/discovery-institute-praises-global-warming-deniers/
33. articles.latimes.com/2011/apr/04/local/la-me-climate-berkeley-20110404
34. www.worldpublicopinion.org/pipa/articles/btenvironmentra/187.php?nid=&id=&pnt=187
35. news.bbc.co.uk/2/hi/in_depth/7010522.stm
36. www.prwatch.org/node/9038
37. www.nytimes.com/2009/08/09/science/earth/09climate.html?hp
38. Epstein, P.R., Mills, E. (Eds.) 2005. *Climate Change Futures: Health, Ecological and Economic Dimensions, Center for Health and the Global Environment*, Harvard Medical School, Boston, MA.

Is Global Warming Really That Bad?

Melissa Denchak

For some people, the idea of an overall warmer climate sounds pleasant and not remotely extreme. However, in this viewpoint, freelance writer and editor Melissa Denchak shows that even a small change in global temperature can have drastic negative consequences.

As you read, consider the following questions:

1. Can you explain one of the potential effects of global warming?
2. What are the consequences of more acidic oceans?
3. Why do higher temperatures result in higher death rates?

Eight degrees Fahrenheit. It may not sound like much—perhaps the difference between wearing a sweater and not wearing one on an early-spring day. But for the world in which we live, which climate experts project will be at least eight degrees warmer by 2100 should global emissions continue on their current path, this small rise will have grave consequences, ones that are already becoming apparent, for every ecosystem and living thing—including us.

According to the National Climate Assessment, human influences are the number one cause of global warming, especially the carbon pollution we cause by burning fossil fuels and the pollution-capturing we prevent by destroying forests. The carbon dioxide, methane, soot, and other pollutants we release into the atmosphere act like a blanket, trapping the sun's heat and causing the planet to warm. Evidence shows that 2000 to 2009 was hotter than any other decade in at least the past 1,300 years. This warming is altering the earth's climate system, including its land, atmosphere, oceans, and ice, in far-reaching ways.

More Frequent and Severe Weather

Higher temperatures are worsening many types of disasters, including storms, heat waves, floods, and droughts. A warmer climate creates an atmosphere that can collect, retain, and drop more water, changing weather patterns in such a way that wet areas become wetter and dry areas drier. "Extreme weather events are costing more and more," says Aliya Haq, deputy director of NRDC's Clean Power Plan initiative. "The number of billion-dollar weather disasters is expected to rise."

According to the National Oceanic and Atmospheric Administration, in 2015 there were 10 weather and climate disaster events in the United States—including severe storms, floods, drought, and wildfires—that caused at least $1 billion in losses. For context, each year from 1980 to 2015 averaged $5.2 billion in disasters (adjusted for inflation). If you zero in on the years between 2011 and 2015, you see an annual average cost of $10.8 billion.

The increasing number of droughts, intense storms, and floods we're seeing as our warming atmosphere holds—and then dumps—more moisture poses risks to public health and safety, too. Prolonged dry spells mean more than just scorched lawns. Drought conditions jeopardize access to clean drinking water, fuel out-of-control wildfires, and result in dust storms, extreme heat events, and flash flooding in the States. Elsewhere around the world, lack of water is a leading cause of death and serious disease. At the opposite end of the spectrum, heavier rains cause streams, rivers, and lakes to overflow, which damages life and property, contaminates drinking water, creates hazardous-material spills, and promotes mold infestation and unhealthy air. A warmer, wetter world is also a boon for food-borne and waterborne illnesses and disease-carrying insects such as mosquitoes, fleas, and ticks.

Higher Death Rates

Today's scientists point to climate change as "the biggest global health threat of the 21st century." It's a threat that impacts all of us—especially children, the elderly, low-income communities, and minorities—and in a variety of direct and indirect ways. As temperatures spike, so does the incidence of illness, emergency room visits, and death.

"There are more hot days in places where people aren't used to it," Haq says. "They don't have air-conditioning or can't afford it. One or two days isn't a big deal. But four days straight where temperatures don't go down, even at night, leads to severe health consequences." In the United States, hundreds of heat-related deaths occur each year due to direct impacts and the indirect effects of heat-exacerbated, life-threatening illnesses, such as heat exhaustion, heatstroke, and cardiovascular and kidney diseases. Indeed, extreme heat kills more Americans each year, on average, than hurricanes, tornadoes, floods, and lightning combined.

Dirtier Air

Rising temperatures also worsen air pollution by increasing ground level ozone, which is created when pollution from cars, factories, and other sources react to sunlight and heat. Ground-level ozone is the main component of smog, and the hotter things get, the more of it we have. Dirtier air is linked to higher hospital admission rates and higher death rates for asthmatics. It worsens the health of people suffering from cardiac or pulmonary disease. And warmer temperatures also significantly increase airborne pollen, which is bad news for those who suffer from hay fever and other allergies.

Higher Wildlife Extinction Rates

As humans, we face a host of challenges, but we're certainly not the only ones catching heat. As land and sea undergo rapid changes, the animals that inhabit them are doomed to disappear if they don't adapt quickly enough. Some will make it, and some won't. According to the Intergovernmental Panel on Climate Change's 2014 assessment, many land, freshwater, and ocean species are shifting their geographic ranges to cooler climes or higher altitudes, in an attempt to escape warming. They're changing seasonal behaviors and traditional migration patterns, too. And yet many still face "increased extinction risk due to climate change." Indeed, a 2015 study showed that vertebrate species—animals with backbones, like fish, birds, mammals, amphibians, and reptiles—are disappearing 114 times faster than they should be, a phenomenon that has been linked to climate change, pollution, and deforestation.

More Acidic Oceans

The Earth's marine ecosystems are under pressure as a result of climate change. Oceans are becoming more acidic, due in large part to their absorption of some of our excess emissions. As this acidification accelerates, it poses a serious threat to underwater life, particularly creatures with calcium carbonate shells or skeletons, including mollusks, crabs, and corals. This can have a huge impact on shellfisheries. Indeed, as of 2015, acidification is believed to have cost the Pacific Northwest oyster industry nearly $110 million. Coastal communities in 15 states that depend on the $1 billion nationwide annual harvest of oysters, clams, and other shelled mollusks face similar long-term economic risks.

Higher Sea Levels

The polar regions are particularly vulnerable to a warming atmosphere. Average temperatures in the Arctic are rising twice as fast as they are elsewhere on earth, and the world's ice sheets are melting fast. This not only has grave consequences for the region's people, wildlife, and plants; its most serious impact may

Global Warming Is Human Caused

Scientists have concluded that most of the observed warming is very likely due to the burning of coal, oil, and gas. This conclusion is based on a detailed understanding of the atmospheric greenhouse effect and how human activities have been tweaking it. …

The atmospheric greenhouse effect naturally keeps our planet warm enough to be livable. Sunlight passes through the atmosphere. Light-colored surfaces, such as clouds or ice caps, radiate some heat back into space. But most of the incoming heat warms the planet's surface. The Earth then radiates some heat back into the atmosphere. Some of that heat is trapped by greenhouse gases in the atmosphere, including carbon dioxide (CO_2).

Human activity—such as burning fossil fuels—causes more greenhouse gases to build up in the atmosphere. As the atmosphere "thickens" with more greenhouse gases, more heat is held in. Fossil fuels such as oil, coal and natural gas are high in carbon and, when burned, produce major amounts of carbon dioxide or CO_2. A single gallon of gasoline, when burned, puts 19 pounds of carbon dioxide into the atmosphere.

The role of atmospheric carbon dioxide (CO_2) in warming the Earth's surface was first demonstrated by Swedish scientist Svante Arrhenius more than 100 years ago. Scientific data have since established that, for hundreds of thousands of years, changes in temperature have closely tracked with atmospheric CO_2 concentrations. Since the Industrial Revolution, the burning of coal, oil and natural gas has emitted roughly 500 billion tons of CO_2, about half of which remains in the atmosphere. This CO_2 is the biggest factor responsible for recent warming trends.

– National Wildlife Federation

be on rising sea levels. By 2100, it's estimated our oceans will be one to four feet higher, threatening coastal systems and low-lying areas, including entire island nations and the world's largest cities, including New York, Los Angeles, and Miami as well as Mumbai, Sydney, and Rio de Janeiro.

There's no question: Climate change promises a frightening future, and it's too late to turn back the clock. We've already taken care of that by pumping a century's worth of pollution into the air nearly unchecked. "Even if we stopped all carbon dioxide emissions tomorrow, we'd still see some effects," Haq says. That, of course, is the bad news. But there's also good news. By aggressively reducing our global emissions now, "we can avoid a lot of the severe consequences that climate change would otherwise bring," says Haq.

How Much of the World Is Responsible for Global Warming?

Anup Shah

In the following viewpoint, GlobalIssues.org creator Anup Shah discusses climate change negotiations and why some countries should bear a greater responsibility for emission reductions and actions than others. He argues that wealthy nations have done more to create climate change than poor nations and that developing countries will be addressing climate change in other ways.

As you read, consider the following questions:

1. Why do rich countries bear a greater responsibility for climate change?
2. According to the Pew Center, what are some of the things that are already being done to alleviate climate change?
3. Why are climate negotiations ignoring social justice and equity?

For a number of years, there have been concerns that climate change negotiations will essentially ignore a key principle of climate change negotiation frameworks: the common but differentiated responsibilities. This recognizes that historically:

- Industrialized nations have emitted far more greenhouse gas emissions than developing nations (even if some developing

"Climate Justice and Equity," by Anup Shah, Global Issues, January 8, 2012, http://www.globalissues.org/article/231/climate-justice-and-equity. Reprinted by permission of the author.

nations are only now increasing theirs) enabling a cheaper path to industrialization;

- Rich countries therefore face the biggest responsibility and burden for action to address climate change; and

- Rich countries therefore must support developing nations adapt to avoid the polluting (i.e. easier and cheaper) path to development—through financing and technology transfer, for example.

This notion of climate justice is typically ignored by many rich nations and their mainstream media, making it easy to blame China, India and other developing countries, or gain credence in the false balancing argument that if they must be subject to emission reductions then so must China and India. There may be a case for emerging nations to be subject to some reduction targets, but the burden of reductions must lie with industrialized countries.

In the meanwhile, rich nations have done very little within the Kyoto Protocol to reduce emissions by any meaningful amount, while they are all for negotiating a follow on treaty that brings more pressure to developing countries to agree to emissions targets.

In effect, the more they delay the more the poor nations will have to save the Earth with their sacrifices (and if it works, as history shows, the rich and powerful will find a way to rewrite history to claim they were the ones that saved the planet).

Why Don't Poor Countries Have Emission Reduction Targets?

"Global warming is primarily a result of the industrialization and motorization levels in the OECD countries, on whom the main onus for mitigation presently lies."

-World Bank, Transport Economics and Sector Policy briefing, quoted from Collision Course; Free trade's free ride on the global climate, New Economics Foundation, November 10, 2000.

It has long been accepted that those industrialized nations that have been industrializing since the Industrial Revolution bear more responsibility for human-induced climate change. This is because greenhouse gases can remain in the atmosphere for decades.

With a bit of historical context then, claims of equity and fairness take on a different meaning than simply suggesting all countries should be reducing emissions by the same amount. But some industrialized nations appear to reject or ignore this premise.

Common Goal but Different Responsibilities

During various stages of climate negotiations, the US complained about the apparent unfairness in the Kyoto Protocol, which doesn't commit developing nations to the same levels of reductions in global warming pollutants.

However, what Washington has not mention is that **the developing nations are NOT the ones who have caused the pollution for the past 150 or so years** and that it would be unfair to ask them to cut back at for the mistakes of the currently industrialized nations.

When the United Nations Framework Convention on Climate Change was formulated and then signed and ratified in 1992 by most of the world's countries (including the United States and other nations who would later back out of the subsequent Kyoto Protocol), the principle of *common but differentiated responsibilities* was acknowledged. In short, this principle recognized that:

> • The largest share of historical and current global emissions of greenhouse gases has originated in developed countries;
> • Per capita emissions in developing countries are still relatively low;
> • The share of global emissions originating in developing countries will grow to meet their social and development needs.
> -The United Nations Framework Convention on Climate Change

That is,

- Today's rich nations are responsible for global warming;

- It is unfair to expect the third world to make emissions reductions in the same way.

- In addition, developing countries will also be tackling climate change in other ways.

These three are discussed further:

Today's rich nations are responsible for global warming

Greenhouse gases tend to remain in the atmosphere for many decades so historical emissions are an important consideration.

[…]

Historically, the rich countries have counted for around 70% of carbon emissions (even though they have represented only 20% of the world's population, approximately).

The United Kingdom (the first empire to industrialize with heavy fossil fuel usage) as well as other European nations have emitted large amounts since their early path to development. Although it became an empire later than most European powers, the sheer size of the United States and its global dominance after World War II made it quickly overtake UK's *total* emissions.

By contrast, the late entry to industrialization for China, India and other developing countries means their cumulative emissions have been far smaller.

Even though more recent media coverage and international meetings concentrate on getting India, China and other developing nations to reduce their emissions before rich countries do more, historical emissions show that the burden should really be on the rich countries.

No doubt, developing nations should be aware of their recent rise and also do more to curb their emissions. But given their later entry to industrialization and that their per capita emissions are even less than rich nations, more emission reduction could also be achieved per person in rich nations.

Greenhouse gases stay in the atmosphere for decades. It is rarely mentioned in Western mainstream media, but has been known for a while, as the Delhi-based *Centre for Science and Environment* (CSE) noted back in 2002:

> "Industrialized countries set out on the path of development much earlier than developing countries, and have been emitting GHGs [Greenhouse gases] in the atmosphere for years without any restrictions. Since GHG emissions accumulate in the atmosphere for decades and centuries, the industrialized countries' emissions are still present in the earth's atmosphere. Therefore, the North is responsible for the problem of global warming given their huge historical emissions. It owes its current prosperity to decades of overuse of the common atmospheric space and its limited capacity to absorb GHGs."
>
> -*Background for COP 8, Center for Science and Environment,*
> *October 25, 2002*

And of course, this was enshrined in the "common but differentiated responsibilities" principle a decade before that.

It is unfair to expect the third world to make emissions reductions to the same level as rich nations

It is therefore unfair to expect the third world to make emissions reductions, especially considering that their development and consumption is (more generally) for basic needs, while for the rich, it has moved on to luxury consumption and associated life styles.

As the above-mentioned *WRI* report also adds: Much of the growth in emissions in developing countries results from the provision of basic human needs for growing populations, while emissions in industrialized countries contribute to growth in a standard of living that is already far above that of the average person worldwide. This is exemplified by the large contrasts in per capita carbons emissions between industrialized and developing countries. Per capita emissions of carbon in the U.S. are over 20 times higher than India, 12 times higher than Brazil and seven times higher than China.

As the above-mentioned *CSE* also adds:

"Developing countries, on the other hand, have taken the road to growth and development very recently. In countries like India, emissions have started growing but their per capita emissions are still significantly lower than that of industrialized countries. The difference in emissions between industrialized and developing countries is even starker when per capita emissions are taken into account. In 1996, for instance, the emission of 1 US citizen equaled that of 19 Indians."

> -*Background for COP 8, Center for Science and Environment,*
> *October 25, 2002*

[...]

(The slight difference in emissions capita quoted by the sources above are due to the differences in the date of the data and the changes that had taken place between.)

Furthermore, many emissions in countries such as India and China are from rich country corporations out-sourcing production to these countries. Products are then exported or sold to the rich. Yet, currently, the blame for such emissions are put on the producer not the consumer. It is not a clear-cut issue though, as some producers create products and try to market them to consumers to buy, while other times, there is a market/ consumer demand for certain products. Companies who can try to avoid more regulation and higher wages in richer countries may attempt to off-shore such production. As discussed on this site's consumption section, some 80% of the world's resources are consumed by the wealthiest 20% of the world (the rich countries). This portion has been higher in the past, suggesting that those countries should therefore bear the brunt of the targets. This issue is discussed in more detail in various parts of this site's trade and economic issues section.

Developing countries will also be tackling climate change in other ways

Under the Convention, the rich were to help provide means

for the developing world to transition to cleaner technologies while developing:

> "The extent to which developing country Parties will effectively implement their commitments under the Convention will depend on the effective implementation by developed country Parties of their commitments under the Convention related to financial resources and transfer of technology and will take fully into account that economic and social development and poverty eradication are the first and overriding priorities of the developing country Parties."
>
> *- The United Nations Framework Convention on*
> *Climate Change*

Furthermore, many developing nations are *already* providing voluntary cuts and as they become larger polluters, they too will be subject to reduction mechanisms.

New Scientist reports that Brazil, China, India and Mexico and other such fast developing countries have slowed their rising greenhouse gas emissions by more than the total cuts demanded of rich nations by the Kyoto Protocol yet this is rarely reported by the mainstream when Bush and others point to China and India concerns.

Policies primarily intended to curb the air pollution from factories and cars or to save energy have had the side effect of fighting global warming. Note, however, the emissions are still rising, but at a much slower rate.

At the end of 2005, *Reuters* reports that a Chinese state-owned energy firm plans to invest at least $2.48 billion over the next five years in biomass, garbage treatment and other alternative energy projects. This company, China Energy Conservation Investment Corp., announced this in response to a new law in China promoting renewable energy, which sets tariffs in favor of non-fossil energy such as wind, water and solar power and is due to take effect in January.

China has a goal of getting 15% of its energy from renewable sources by 2020, though the same report admits that China still largely depends on coal for its electricity (some 70%) and will continue to do so.

Compare that, however, to say, an industrialized country that feels it is taking a lead in climate change affairs: United Kingdom's goal is for 10% of all its electricity to be from renewable sources.

At the end of 2009, *Reuters* also reported on a new Chinese law requiring power grid operators to buy all the electricity that is produced by renewable energy generators, increasing the proportion of energy that comes from renewable sources, with harsh fines for failure to comply.

US News & World Report adds that China's renewable energy market is expected to grow to $100 billion over the next 15 years.

A 2002 report from the *Pew Center* for example, highlights how key developing nations have been able to significantly reduce their combined greenhouse gas emissions by some 19 percent, or 300 million tons a year, with possibly another 300 million tons by 2010. Those nations are Brazil, China, India, Mexico, South Africa, and Turkey.

Various efforts reported by *Pew* included:

- Market and energy reforms to promote economic growth;

- Development of alternative fuels to reduce energy imports;

- Aggressive energy efficiency programs;

- Use of solar and other renewable energy to raise living standards in rural locations;

- Reducing deforestation;

- Slowing population growth; and

- Switching from coal to natural gas to diversify energy sources and reduce air pollution.

This shows that the rich nations can and should be able to do so as well.

An earlier report in 2000 from the *WRI* also notes that developing countries are *already* taking action to limit emissions.

In a report, earlier still (1999), *WRI* also noted that:

- Growth caps for the poor amount to guessing on a country's future economic performance;

- Modeling developing country climate change commitments after industrialized country commitments is not the way to go, and could threaten the environmental integrity of the Kyoto Protocol, given the uncertainty of future emission levels and the international emissions trading provisions in the Protocol.

- For poorer countries, an alternative policy may therefore be appropriate (and WRI goes on to suggest one).

What Might a Fair Share of Emissions Look Like?

Martin Khor notes the historically large amount of emissions from rich nations that have helped them develop.

Assuming by 2050 that 600 gigatons of carbon emissions is the limit that needs to be reached to prevent climate change getting worse, Khor looked at fairer allocation of emissions based on per capita emissions, taking into account what has already been emitted by rich countries (Annex 1) and non-Annex 1 countries (i.e the rest of the world).

Noting that rich countries have already had their chance to develop and emitted more in than their fair share in the process, is there a way to redress so the end result is equitable for *all*?

A fairer allocation is possible while allowing poorer countries to develop but would require the rich countries to cut back significantly.

By 2008, the rich nations had already counted for the majority of carbon emissions, since 1800: 240 gigatons (Gt), vs 91 Gt from the rest of the world.

But it is likely that emissions by 2050 will mean rich countries have ended up using some 325 Gt (of the 600 total that is aimed for), or just over 50%. Yet, it needs to be around 20% (because the rich nations are roughly 20% of the population).

The 20% allocation could be achieved if rich countries accept they owe a carbon debt which would also allow the rest of the world to develop.

Khor describes the notion of negative emissions which includes knowledge and technology sharing with developing nations to help them combat climate change.

It now seems unfair on *rich* countries! They now have to cut their emissions significantly *and* help finance poor countries' to emit more! But there is a logic to this:

• The polluting ways the industrialized nations used to industrialize is not to be encouraged for the rest of the world.

• Those polluting ways are also considered the cheaper, or easier way to develop, which, as the *Centre for Science and Environment* noted earlier, was akin to free-riding on the atmospheric commons.

• Given this low-hanging fruit is not encouraged for developing countries, their path to development requires more costly measures.

• Given industrialized nations have used up most of the low-hanging fruit, it seems fair that they help developing countries down an alternative path (which would still lead to economic benefits for industrialized nations because they would likely be leaders in developing such technology required by developing nations).

In some ways, the above numbers are simplistic and generalized. For example:

• Not all of today's industrialized nations were necessarily industrialized in the past (though many were)

• Population ratios may have changed in this time period so such factors would need to be brought in to create more accurate numbers.

- Also, in the past industrialized nations have emitted greenhouse gases while producing items used by others around the world. (Although, industrialized nations have, for many years, consumed more resources compared to developing countries than they do today so have often produced for themselves more than for the poorer countries.)

- This producing for others also happens today. China for example, claims around one third of its production is for consumption by the rich part of the world, and there is more globalization today than in the past whereby poorer nations are encouraged to create exports for richer nations.

As crude and high-level as the actual numbers may be, it highlights that social justice and equity issues have been ignored from climate negotiations and from mainstream media discussions in the industrialized world, allowing views such as needing China and India to make drastic cuts more palatable than should be, perhaps.

Climate Negotiations Ignoring Social Justice and Equity

The above, and other principles in the Convention, formed what some described as the **social justice and equity** part of climate change issues. Unfortunately these have been largely ignored in the discussions which are usually dominated by the rich nations, and oil producing countries, who talk more about **economic effectiveness** only. In a way, this can be understood, because:

- Rich nations such as the United States, and OPEC countries, are worried about the economic impact of changing the fundamental underpinnings of their economies and their way of life.

- The social justice and equity dimension is a concern primarily for the third world. Without as strong a voice as the rich countries, when it comes to discussion and negotiation, this concern isn't heard, understood, or seen as important.

Hence, when the US backed out of the Kyoto agreements on emission reductions citing, amongst other things, that China and India for example should also have emissions cuts imposed on them, these social justice and equity dimensions were hardly considered, or treated as important enough. But considering the following:

- Meaningful assistance to other countries to transition to cleaner development has been lacking;

- Third world debt and poverty has diverted immense resources from sustainable development;

- Poor countries including China and India had already made reasonable emission cuts;

- Pressure from citizens in rich countries to clean up their environment has often actually led to moving those dirty industries/factories to the third world while still producing for the benefit or profit for the first world. This was eventually noted by the BBC, in December 2005, reporting on new research that shows similar fears, despite these concerns being voiced many years ago.

These and many, many other related issues have hardly received detailed coverage either at all, or at least at the same time as the coverage of US reasons for backing out of Kyoto. Hence it is understandable why many US citizens would agree with the Bush Administration's position on this, for example.

Rich Nations Have Outsourced Their Carbon Emissions

Global trade is an important feature of the modern world. The production and global distribution of manufactured products thus form a large portion of global human carbon emissions.

The Kyoto Protocol assigns carbon emissions to countries based on where production takes place rather than where things are consumed.

For many years, critics of the Kyoto Protocol have long argued that this means rich countries, who have outsourced much of their manufacturing to developing nations have an accounting trick they can use to show more emissions reduction than developing nations. The above-mentioned *BBC* article noted back in 2005 that this outsourcing had taken place, but the idea of doing this came way before the Kyoto Protocol came into being.

In 1991 Larry Summers, then Chief Economist for the World Bank (and US Treasury Secretary, in the Clinton Administration, until George Bush and the Republican party came into power), had been a strong backer of structural adjustment policies. He wrote in an internal memo:

"Just between you and me, shouldn't the World Bank be encouraging more migration of dirty industries to the LDCs [less developed countries]?... The economic logic behind dumping a load of toxic waste in the lowest wage country is impeccable, and we should face up to that... Under-populated countries in Africa are vastly under-polluted; their air quality is probably vastly inefficiently low compared to Los Angeles or Mexico City... The concern over an agent that causes a one in a million change in the odds of prostate cancer is obviously going to be much higher in a country where people survive to get prostate cancer than in a country where under-five mortality is 200 per thousand."

-Lawrence Summers, Let them eat pollution, The Economist, February 8, 1992. Quoted from Vandana Shiva, Stolen Harvest, (South End Press, 2000) p.65; See also Richard Robbins, Global Problems and the Culture of Capitalism (Allyn and Bacon, 1999), pp. 233-236 for a detailed look at this.

Although the discussion above wasn't about carbon emissions, the intention was the same: rather than directly address the problem, off-shoring dirty industries to the developing nations and let them deal with it.

More recently, *The Guardian* provided a useful summary of the impacts of this approach: carbon emissions cuts by developed countries since 1990 have been canceled out by increases in imported goods from developing countries—many times over.

They were summarizing global figures compiled and published in the Proceedings of the National Academy of Sciences of the US. And the findings seemed to vindicate what many environmental groups had said for many years about the Kyoto Protocol as noted earlier.

In more detail:

"According to standard data, developed countries can claim to have reduced their collective emissions by almost 2% between 1990 and 2008. But once the carbon cost of imports have been added to each country, and exports subtracted—the true change has been an increase of 7%. If Russia and Ukraine—which cut their CO_2 emissions rapidly in the 1990s due to economic collapse—are excluded, the rise is 12%.

...

Much of the increase in emissions in the developed world is due to the US, which promised a 7% cut under Kyoto but then did not to ratify the protocol. Emissions within its borders increased by 17% between 1990 and 2008—and by 25% when imports and exports are factored in.

In the same period, UK emissions fell by 28 million tonnes, but when imports and exports are taken into account, the domestic footprint has risen by more than 100 million tonnes. Europe achieved a 6% cut in CO_2 emissions, but when outsourcing is considered that is reduced to 1%.

...

The study shows a very different picture for countries that export more carbon-intensive goods than they import. China, whose growth has been driven by export-based industries, is usually described as the world's largest emitter of CO_2, but its footprint drops by almost a fifth when its imports and exports are taken into account, putting it firmly behind the US. China alone accounts for a massive 75% of the developed world's offshored emissions, according to the paper."

-Duncan Clark, Carbon cuts by developed countries cancelled out by imported goods, The Guardian, April 25, 2011

Politics and Interests

At the time of the end of the CoP-8 climate change conference, what appears to be a change in principle by the European Union, towards the position of the developing countries has emerged. That is, as Centre for Science and Environment (CSE) comments, Denmark, currently president of the European Union, announced yesterday [October 31, 2002] that developing countries would not get any money for adapting to climate change until they start discussing reduction commitments. Not only can this be described as blackmail, as CSE also highlight, but in addition, rich nations themselves have shied away from their commitments, amounting to hypocrisy.

As CSE continued, Adaptation funds have been on the negotiations agenda for several years now. Industrialized countries, including progressive countries like Denmark, have run away from committing anything concrete, and developing countries have not been able to pin down any liability on them. (CSE has also been critical of leaders in developing countries who are equally to blame for encouraging the perception that they can be bought appearing to respond to money only such, giving an opportunity for some rich nations to exploit that.)

Economics and political agendas always makes it difficult to produce a treaty that all nations can agree to easily. The wealthier and more powerful nations are naturally able to exert more political clout and influence. The US, for example, has pushed for different solutions that will allow it to maintain its dominance. An example of that is trading in emissions, which has seen a number of criticisms.

The way current climate change negotiations have been going unfortunately suggests the developed world will position themselves to use the land of the developing and poor nations to further their own emissions reduction, while leaving few such easy options for the South, as summarized by the following as well:

"Investments in 'carbon sinks' (such as large-scale tree plantations) in the South would result in land being used at the expense of local people, accelerate deforestation, deplete water resources and increase poverty. Entitling the North to buy cheap emission credits from the South, through projects of an often exploitative nature, constitutes 'carbon colonialism.' Industrialised countries and their corporations will harvest the 'low-hanging fruit' (the cheapest credits), saddling Southern countries with only expensive options for any future reduction commitments they might be required to make."

-Saving the Kyoto Protocol Means Ending the Market Mania,
Corporate Europe Observatory, July 2001

In Southeast Asia, Cutting Greenhouse Gases Is Vital to Survival

Murray Hiebert

The historic Paris Climate Summit took place in November 2015, and many participating countries pledged to reduce their greenhouse gas emissions. In this viewpoint, Murray Hiebert, senior adviser and deputy director of the Southeast Asia Program at the Center for Strategic & International Studies, shows how many nations in Southeast Asia are paying attention to the goals and the results of the summit.

As you read, consider the following questions:

1. What did the participating countries pledge to do at the Paris summit?
2. What country was identified as having suffered the most from climate change in the last twenty years?
3. What did Microsoft chairman Bill Gates pledge to do?

Much of the focus at the Paris climate summit that began on November 30 will be on the delegations from the United States, China, and India, and the pledges of the world's largest greenhouse gas emitters to limit emissions, protect forests, and

"Southeast Asian Nations Watch Paris for Deal to Cut Greenhouse Gases," by Murray Hiebert, December 4, 2015. Reprinted by permission. CogitAsia, The Center for Strategic & International Studies (CSIS) Asia Policy Blog. https://www.cogitasia.com/.

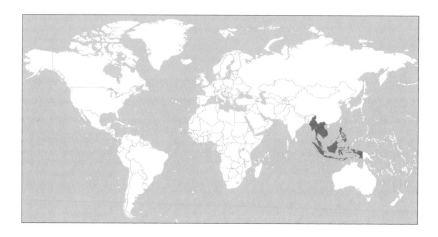

launch rigorous renewable energy projects. Countries in Southeast Asia, several of which are among the most vulnerable to the impact of climate change, are watching closely to see if the nearly 200 participating countries put forward action plans robust enough to pull the world away from its trajectory toward perilous levels of global warming.

Whether a deal to curtail greenhouse gases is achieved depends at least in part on overcoming differences about funding. Many developing countries, led by India and including Indonesia, Malaysia, and others, say that developed nations that have emitted the lion's share of carbon dioxide on their march to industrialization must do more to support the switch to more green energy and assist poorer nations in coping with the impact of climate change.

The Philippines, which is ranked in a 2011 report by the United Nations University's Institute for Environment and Human Security as the third most-at-risk nation from climate change, is committed at the summit to press for stronger global cooperation to limit the destructive effects of climate change. Philippine negotiators will highlight the country's experiences with extreme weather disturbances such as Typhoon Haiyan, which ravaged the Philippines two years ago, to demonstrate the effects of climate change on vulnerable nations. Due to climate change, tropical storms that slam the country up to 10 times a year are expected to increase in intensity.

The Paris summit will seek to cobble together an international climate accord that will aim to limit global warming to about 2 degrees Celsius. The Philippines and other nations that already face the harshest impact of climate change are pushing for a more ambitious and legally binding agreement that will impose a 1.5-degree ceiling. The Philippine government said it aims to cut its carbon emissions by as much as 70 percent by 2030 if it can receive adequate financial and technical assistance.

Indonesia, currently the world's fourth-largest emitter due to its conversion of forest and carbon-rich peat land into agricultural fields, has said it will reduce its emissions by 28 percent by 2030 using its own resources, which would require a sharp reduction in deforestation and forest fires. But Jakarta adds that it would increase this reduction to 41 percent with international assistance. The government also rolled out new regulations banning further exploitation of peat land ahead of the Paris summit. The peat fires that have burned in Indonesia for the past few months have discharged so much carbon dioxide into the atmosphere that Indonesia this year went from the world's sixth- to the world's fourth-largest emitter in the span of six weeks, according to data released in October by the Washington-based World Resources Institute. Deforestation, mostly to create palm oil plantations that produce vegetable oil, causes more pollution than the country's power plants and cars combined.

Vietnam, one of the most densely populated countries in Southeast Asia, is among the world's 11 countries most vulnerable to the effects of climate change, especially floods, droughts, and sea-level increases, according to a UN Environment Program report. Weather-related disasters are estimated to cost around 1.5 percent of the country's gross domestic product (GDP) each year. Rising sea levels are expected to have a devastating impact on Vietnam's rice basket in the fertile Mekong Delta.

Vietnam has pledged to cut its greenhouse emissions by 8 percent by 2030 using domestic resources and up to 25 percent with international help. Under the UN Reducing Emissions from Deforestation and Degradation Program (REDD) program, which Vietnam joined in 2011, it aims to reduce total emissions in the agricultural sector by 20 percent and increase the national level of forest cover to about 45 percent by 2020.

Myanmar was identified as the country most affected by climate change during the 20-year period ending in 2013, according to the UN Risk Model. Cyclone Nargis in 2008 caused at least 140,000 deaths in the Irrawaddy Delta, Myanmar's rice bowl. Myanmar is being deforested at an alarming rate, having lost about 18 percent of its forests between 1990 and 2005 due to commercial logging and expansion of farmland, according to the UN-REDD program.

The long-isolated country, which launched reforms toward free market principles and a transition to democracy in 2011, actually sequesters more greenhouse gases than it emits, but this is expected to change rapidly as the country sets up more power and manufacturing plants and imports more vehicles. Myanmar pledged to the global summit to calculate a reliable estimate for how much it can reduce emissions, and to increase its primary forested area to 30 percent by 2030, up from 10 percent at present.

Thailand is one of 16 countries at "extreme risk" from climate change due to its long coastline. Thailand blames climate change for serious droughts and for the disruptive 2011 floods, which caused an estimated 0.52 percent drop in GDP. Bangkok has pledged to reduce greenhouse gas emissions by 20 percent by 2030 on its own and by an additional 5 percent with increased access to technology transfers and financing from richer nations.

As the summit opened in Paris, it was clear that some big obstacles have to be overcome before a deal can be struck. For starters, the agreement must be accepted unanimously by the almost-200 countries participating before it can be legally binding. One of the biggest challenges could come from the developing nations' grouping, which has insisted that their countries should not be pressed to curtail economic growth to repair a problem that was caused mostly by developed countries. They insist that emissions cuts must be accompanied by billions of dollars of investment to assist developing nations in their shift from fossil fuel to cleaner energy options.

Negotiators were joined in Paris by a group of billionaires, including Microsoft founder Bill Gates, who announced major donations to help reduce emissions, develop alternative sources of energy, and aid developing countries that will be most affected by climate change. Conference organizers hope that commitment from the business community, coupled with the pledge by 20 countries, including the United States, to double their investments in new energy technology to $20 billion over the next five years, will convince developing countries that they will get critical assistance in moving their economies away from carbon dependence.

Southeast Asian leaders hope that by the time the summit winds up on December 11, negotiators will have hammered out a deal to curb greenhouse gases and put together an aid package to help the most vulnerable countries in the region cope with the effects of climate change.

Whose Fault Is Climate Change?

Frank Thomas

One of the most frequently rehashed controversies concerning the issue of climate change is whether it is caused by human activity or is a natural cycle. In the following viewpoint, journalist Frank Thomas explores some of the arguments on both sides of the issue.

As you read, consider the following questions:

1. What is the long-term trend in global warming?
2. What is meant by the term "voodoo science"?
3. What did the research on climate change and pollution teach the author?

The UN Intergovernmental Panel on Climate Change (IPCC) has been around for 25 years. In their report released last Friday, IPCC data surprisingly suggested a "15 year pause" in climate warming ... a cooling period perhaps not too dissimilar to what occurred before in 1965-79.

This view comes from a one-year 60% increase in Arctic sea ice coverage between September 1, 2012 and August 31, 2013. Of course, this fires up the endless debate on how much global average temperatures have risen (and will rise) due to human-induced greenhouse gas (GHG) emissions and how much due to natural variability.

"Is Climate Change Caused by Human Activity or by Natural Cyclical Phenomena?" by Frank Thomas, SanDiegoFreePress.org, October 1, 2013. Reprinted by permission.

Climate research experts agree that there has been a stagnation in global warming since 2000. Increased release of GHG emissions in the 1980s and 1990s led to a new atmospheric high of 400 ppm vs 310 ppm in 1962. An entirely possible 500 ppm GHG concentration or more in the next 40 years spells severe survival problems for all life.

Even though global warming has slowed in recent years, the long term trend is clear: the annual average rate of increase in atmospheric CO_2 has been going up steadily decade to decade—more than doubling at 2.1 ppm per year for the last 10 years vs 0.9 ppm per year 50 years ago! Statistical variations may suggest a temporary cooling effect, but the long term trend largely due to GHG emissions is for more global warming.

The sharp contrast with the stagnation in average earth temperature increases over the last 12 years and the expected cooling down over the next 15 years has climate change skeptics crying "lies" to predictions that CO_2 pollution is the cause of climate change. Nevertheless, ice-free Arctic summers could occur as early as 2014. The Arctic permafrost could disappear in 5 years. An ecologically calamitous earth-warming of 2 degrees Celsius or more—accelerated by a potentially massive release of Arctic methane—could envelop planet earth by 2050.

"RUBBISH" say the skeptics! Some climate historians see the IPCC recent "cooling pause" data as just more evidence that Arctic ice levels are cyclical. In short, they are mainly due to natural variability and not to human activities. Climate-warming and change deniers point to the huge ice meltdown in the 1920s and 1930s ... followed by an intense ocean ice recovery that ended in 1979 ... followed by a repeat huge Arctic ice meltdown in 1980s and 1990s ... followed by IPCC's modeling data now spelling a 15 year pause in Arctic ice meltdown. This "return of the Arctic ice sheet" and climate effect has been discussed in a crisis IPCC top meeting in Stockholm which concluded just a few days ago.

The haunting questions remain: What's happening with the Arctic ice and its ice-captured gigantic reserves of CO_2 and especially CH_4 (methane)?

How certain is it that humans are causing climate warming and the resultant climate change? Notwithstanding the cyclical trend noted above, the IPCC still says it is "95% confident that global warming has been caused by humans and will continue to be caused by humans" … unless drastic action is taken on reducing the deadly greenhouse gas emissions from methane and fossil fuels.

A very brief historical overview follows of the IPCC's previous four reports on disturbing trends in global climate warming and change … trends that continue to be treated as simply pure climate science nonsense and deception by hard-core skeptics.

Brief Overview of Reports of Intergovernmental Panel on Climate Change (IPCC) Since 1990 and Reactions

• In its first 1990 REPORT, the IPCC refrained from suggesting that the 0.5 degrees Celsius rise in the average global earth temperature since the start of the 20th century was due to humans or from natural variability.

• In its second 1995 REPORT, the IPCC did not move much from its earlier position of the origin of higher global temperatures. However, it did say that subsequent research since the last report gave a strong indication that, "The balance of evidence suggests a discernible human influence on the global climate."

• In its third 2001 REPORT, the IPCC went a step further when saying the continuing trends in climate warming were "likely"—meaning more than a 66% chance of being due to humans.

• In its fourth 2007 REPORT, the "likely" scientific viewpoint got much stronger with the term "very likely"—meaning more than a 90% chance of being due to humans. Conclusions were more definitive that the warming up was unmistakable from measurements of atmosphere and ocean temperatures, from worldwide rapid melting of glaciers and pole ice and from the rise in sea level.

The provocative statement was also made that, even if the greenhouse gas effect stabilized, the warming up of the earth and the rising sea levels could continue for a 100 years with irreversible effects on nature and humans. As noted, not surprisingly, the neo-conservative Tea Party types call this "voodoo" science and lies, playing on fears of traditional fossil fuel, auto and chemical industry polluters that they will be faced with the unnecessary huge costs of going green.

The British newspaper, the Guardian, wrote that the conservative American Enterprise Institute offered $10,000 and a very generous out-of-pocket compensation for any article written by a scientist that brought the credibility of the IPCC in doubt.

In 2009, the neo-conservative outcry achieved new levels when in effect criminal actions were taken to discredit the climate science represented by IPCC and other credible climate science organizations.

Just before a meeting of top climate people in Copenhagen in 2009, "CLIMATEGATE" broke out. Thousands of e-mails of climate researchers were stolen and published by anonymous hackers who accused the science community of a plot to manipulate climate data. Nothing fraudulent was found.

But the Copenhagen meeting ended postponing indefinitely discussions of ideas and actions to save the world from climate over-warming. A year later in 2010, a careless mistake occurred in IPCC's 2007 REPORT. It was discovered on page 492 in the second part of the three part REPORT, each part of which contained about a thousand pages! On page 492 the statement was made that all of Himalaya's thousands of glaciers will be melted by 2035.

Further, it was thought that when the ice melted, 1.5 billion people below would be without drinking water from the many Himalayan rivers. In a Science report of June 2012, Dutch researchers learned that most rivers in the area were NOT dependent on melted ice water since much rain water falls into the rivers each year. So, as the Dutch report concluded, Himalayan drinking water availability for the next 100 years is not at risk.

The IPCC failed to help themselves by immediately admitting to the error and correcting it. Instead the reaction was arrogant and slow. Recently, IPCC's Chairman had this to say in a Dutch internet interview:

"We were confronted with an organized attack. No one knew how we must react. We had no communication strategy ... Science is one expertise, communication is another ... We were naïve and in any event not very efficient. The climate 'doubter' promoters have much money. The Chairman of IPCC is not paid. We are an organization that works with 2000 to 3000 scientists and that has 800 writers for the REPORTS—all not paid."

(SOURCES: Reports of IPCC; NRC Weekend, "Negotiations Over the Climate," Sept. 21/22, 2013; NRC, "The Analysis of the Environment is Becoming More Precise," by P. Luttikhuis, Sept. 23, 2013)

Needless to say, this and recent news about a 12-month 60% increase in Arctic ice coverage has been fertile grounds for climate-denier critics of how the IPCC operates and its very existence. IPCC has since asked for advice from an independent commission, The Interacademy Council.

Under the leadership of Robert Dijkgraaf, a study conclusion is that the IPCC has grown inadequately with the pace of environmental developments and has operated amateurishly. It's not always clear who speaks for the organization or when scientists are giving their own meaning or are speaking for the IPCC.

This critique, among others, has been addressed in the upcoming fifth REPORT of the IPCC. Important organizational changes have already been made. Recently, its Chairman, Jean-Pascal Van Ypersele came forth with interesting clarifications to allay the confusion about IPCC's functions:

"We do not write policy. Our mission is to be 'policy relevant.' This we do by laying out choices, pluses and minuses, limits and costs. It has been asserted that the IPCC has said the average global temperature must NOT exceed 2 degrees Celsius. BUT, we have never said that. We have exposed the risks if the temperature increases 1 degree Celsius or 2 degrees. But we do not determine which choice should be made. Never! Never!

"The climate of the last 10,000 years has been very stable. Now we are talking of a temperature increase of 1 degree to 6 degrees Celsius in less than 100 years. That is unbelievable, an enormous change in climate! Many policy-makers underestimate the scale of the changes we will experience in the next 100 years. So it's frustrating that, even when the diagnosis is getting more precise, we make such slow progress on implementing rules to protect the planet."

Summary

The brings me back to the essential question: How certain is it that climate warming is human caused?

U.S. climate expert, Prof. Judith Curry, strongly faults the IPCC forecast models as being too sensitive to CO_2 as the root cause of climate warming.

She omits the overwhelming supporting evidence of fossil fuel pollution and related positive feedback effects in breaking down sub-sea ice clathrates containing massive amounts of methane. The ongoing serious acidification of oceans (particularly from burning very dirty coal), the resultant destroying of microscopic phytoplankton that supplies most of our planet's life oxygen and the continuing high rates of deforestation due in part to forest fires contribute significantly to reduced CO_2 absorption.

Scientists have confirmed that the oceans are turning into acid 10 times faster than they were 300 million years ago during the biggest mass extinction event in earth history. Prof. Curry apparently sees no relationship whatsoever between climate warming and a historical 50 year CO_2 growing proliferation in the atmosphere to a concentration of 400 ppm ... a consistent curve upward from a mild annual rate of increase of 0.90 ppm/year during 1963-1972 to a shocking 2.07 ppm/year 2003-2012.

She seems to be a believer that historically CO_2 levels have increased FOLLOWING a global warming event rather than PRECEDING a global warming event and causing it. As well as being a myth over the past 50 years, this thinking has long been a myth used to explain environmental extinctions occurring millions of years ago—the latter has just been credibly shown to be FALSE by a French research team.

Today, the scientific proof is overwhelming that heat trapping CO_2 acceleration in the atmosphere plus the related positive feedbacks are the primary cause of intensified climate warming. This ecologically destructive dynamic is going to be super-accelerated by CHINA and INDIA's 2.5 billion people, 98% of whom earn less than $2,000 a year plus another 2 billion population increase mostly in undeveloped countries. This represents over 4.5 billion people living in mostly relatively un-industrialized, low standard of living countries who will eventually naturally want to have many of the material possessions—or should I say material obsessions—expected by people in the more maturely developed countries.

These interrelated demographic, living standard developments combined with the pollution from fossil fuels and the positive feedback loop factors are seriously compounding climate warming problems.

This is unaddressed by Prof. Curry and summed up with the vague and empty epithet, "Uncertainty is getting bigger" … concerning the role of these factors in increasing unstable climate warming. Furthermore, and most importantly, the 60% Arctic ice increase in the last 12 months was already expected by climate scientists, most of whom say this statistic is largely irrelevant (see: Guardian Climate Consensus—"The 97%," by Dana Nucciteli) because:

> "Arctic ice generally reaches its minimum in September and scientists had already predicted LESS MELT for this year compared to last year. The reason so many climate scientists predicted more ice this year than last is quite simple. There's a principle in statistics known as the 'regression toward the mean,' which is the phenomenon that if an extreme value of a variable is observed, the next measurement will generally be less extreme. In other words, we should not often expect to observe records in consecutive years. The year 2012 shattered the previous record

low sea ice extent; hence 'regression to the mean' told us that 2013 would likely have a higher minimum extent."

The Arctic sea ice minimum is the day usually in September when the sea ice is at its smallest extent (coverage). BUT, the National Snow and Ice Data Center(NSIDC) points out that the currently high Arctic sea ice September coverage is still well BELOW the 1981 to 2010 average for the month. In words of NSIDC director, Mark Serreze, "While today's coverage is a welcome recovery from last year's record low, the overall trend is still decidedly downwards." NSIDC officials further pointed out:

> "Sea ice extent for August 2013 averaged 6.09 million sq. kilometers (2.35 million sq. miles). This was 1.03 sq. kilometers (308,000 sq. miles) BELOW the 1981 to 2010 average for August, but well ABOVE the level recorded last year, which was the lowest September ice extent in the satellite record. Ice extent this August was similar to the years from 2008 to 2010. These contrasts in ice extent from one year to the next highlight the year-to-year variability attending the overall, long-term decline in sea ice extent."

As usual figures can be misleading and downright misused, especially when the multi-faceted environmental pollution picture I've summarized is not taken into account. I certainly have an open mind as to how much greenhouse gas emissions are due to carbon dioxide and potentially to Arctic methane versus how much is due to natural variability (non-human caused).

Professional research on climate change and pollution to date convince this investigative reporter that the climate warming course of the last 30-40 years is human caused … and will become increasingly human caused by a 7 billion world population, rising to 9 billion by 2050. Excluding North America and Europe, the world population comprises over 85% of quasi-developed and developing nations – nearly 40% from China and India alone! That's a lot of heat trapping CO_2 and CH_4 coming into the atmosphere!

The risks to Mother Earth are simply too great to gamble on a "life as usual" acceptance of a potentially massive ecological and human extermination event—especially knowing the speed and scale of the CO_2 and CH_4 pollution trend line we are now on. Placing all bets and blame on cycles and natural variability for the obvious human disproportionate disturbance of nature's environmental balance on the only planet known to harbor human life … is a bet we should all pass on for the sake of our children's children and their children's children.

Postscript:

Concerning the just published IPCC REPORT, the following was reported in the *International Herald Tribune* today (September 28-29):

> *"Within three decades scientists warn, warming could be irreversible. The world's top climate scientists on Friday formally embraced an upper limit on greenhouse gases for the first time … establishing a target level at which humanity must stop spewing them into the atmosphere or face catastrophic climate changes. Scientists warned the target was likely to be exceeded in a matter of decades unless steps were taken soon to reduce emissions. The experts cited a litany of changes already under way, warned they were likely to accelerate and expressed virtual certainty that human activity was the main cause."*

So much for the exaggerated, unfounded reactions by die-hard climate change skeptics! The recent revelation of a 60% increase in the Arctic ice cap over the last 12 months does NOT support "the doubters and deniers" propaganda that climate change is thus inherently NOT human caused … that it is a cycle and a fluctuation process naturally caused which has existed for millions of years!

Periodical and Internet Sources Bibliography

The following articles have been selected to supplement the diverse views presented in this chapter.

The Economist, "Is It Global Warming or Just the Weather?" May 9, 2015. http://www.economist.com/news/international/21650552 -scientists-are-getting-more-confident-about-attributing -heatwaves-and-droughts-human.

Daniel Huber and Jay Gulledge, "Extreme Weather and Climate Change," Center for Climate and Energy Solutions, December 2011. http://www.c2es.org/publications/extreme-weather-and -climate-change.

David Kreutzer, "Five Myths About Extreme Weather and Global Warming," *The Daily Signal*, March 31, 2013. http://www .dailysignal.com/2014/03/31/five-myths-extreme-weather -global-warming.

Tim McDonnell, "The Link Between Human-Caused Climate Change and Extreme Weather Events," *Newsweek*, November 5, 2015. http://www.newsweek.com/climate-change-extreme-weather -events-wildfires-droughts-391116.

National Wildlife Federation, "Global Warming and Extreme Weather." http://www.nwf.org/Wildlife/Threats-to-Wildlife/Global -Warming/Global-Warming-is-Causing-Extreme-Weather.aspx.

Skeptical Science, "Is Extreme Weather Caused by Global Warming?" http://www.skepticalscience.com/extreme-weather-global -warming-intermediate.htm.

Missy Stultz, "Climate Change Is Happening Now—Here's Eight Things We Can Do to Adapt to It," *The Guardian* (UK), March 21, 2017.

James Taylor, "NOAA Report Destroys Global Warming Link to Extreme Weather," *Forbes*, October 9, 2014.

Justin Worland, "Scientists Are Making Stronger Links Between Climate Change and Extreme Weather," *Time*, March 11, 2016. http://time.com/4255428/climate-change-extreme-weather.

Yale Environment 360, "Forum: Is Extreme Weather Linked to Global Warming?" http://e360.yale.edu/features/forum_is_extreme_ weather_linked_to_global_warming.

Eric Zerkel, "Human-Caused Global Warming Contributed to Weather Extremes: Report," September 30, 2014. http://weather .com/science/environment/news/report-human-caused-climate -change-2013-weather-extremes-20140929.

GLOBALVIEWPOINTS

CHAPTER 4

Coping with Extreme Weather

How Various Countries Are Tackling Climate Change

NPR News Staff

Climate change is already affecting most parts of the world. In this viewpoint, National Public Radio, a widely respected national news organization, reports on climate change in different places and what those countries are doing to deal with immediate problems and plan for the future.

As you read, consider the following questions:

1. What is Brazil doing about deforestation?
2. Can you name one requirement of the Kyoto Protocol?
3. What two countries won't commit to reducing carbon emissions?

While nations wrangle over a new global treaty on climate change, the question on many minds is: What happens next? Key portions of the Kyoto Protocol are set to expire at the end of 2012. But many of the world's major greenhouse gas emitters have already set national targets to reduce emissions, and they're forging their own initiatives to meet those goals.

Some are focusing on curbing deforestation and boosting renewable energy sources. Several nations are experimenting with cap-and-trade plans: Regulators set mandatory limits on industrial emissions, but companies that exceed those "caps" can buy permits to emit from companies that have allowances to spare. In some cases, it's not clear that countries are doing much to meet their stated climate goals. What *is* clear is that the pledges currently on the table aren't legally binding, and they fall far short of what would be required to stabilize the planet's atmosphere.

Here's a look at what nations are doing:

Australia

*Australia has set a national goal of reducing greenhouse gas emissions by **5 percent below 2000 levels by 2020.***

Australia didn't sign onto the Kyoto Protocol until 2007, after its Labor Party took control of government, reversing the previous administration's policy. Under the climate pact, Australia agreed to hold the growth in its greenhouse gas emissions to 8 percent above 1990 levels for the 2008-2012 period. By and large, Australia has met those targets, mostly by reducing deforestation and land clearing.

In November 2011, Australian lawmakers approved an ambitious carbon trading plan—the world's largest outside of Europe. Under the plan, Australia's 500 worst polluters would be forced to pay a tax on every ton of carbon they emit starting in July 2012. By 2015, the nation plans to move to a full-on, market-based carbon trading system. Australia says it plans to link its carbon market to one set up in neighboring New Zealand. That might make it harder to dismantle the market if conservatives win back control of Australia's government in 2013.

Brazil

*Brazil is aiming to reduce its **emissions to 1994 levels and cut deforestation by 80 percent** from historic highs by 2020.*

Brazil's National Climate Change Plan is focused on expanding renewable electric energy sources and beefing up the use of biofuels in the transportation industry. The country is also focusing heavily on reducing deforestation rates: It's hoping to eliminate illegal deforestation and bring the net loss of forest coverage to zero by 2015.

But a proposal to loosen Brazil's deforestation rules is currently making its way through the legislature. If enacted, critics say the changes could create more opportunities for logging.

Canada

*When Canada signed onto the Kyoto Protocol, it committed to reducing its greenhouse gas emissions by 6 percent below 1990 levels. It later proposed a new, less ambitious goal to reduce emissions by **17 percent from 2005 levels by 2020**, a pledge that matches the U.S.*

Canada did little to try to meet its obligations under the Kyoto Protocol. Indeed, today, the country's emissions are 17 percent above 1990 levels—in large part because of emissions tied to the dirty business of extracting oil from Alberta's tar sands.

According to a Canadian government report released in mid-2011, emissions from tar sands will more than cancel out the progress that Canada has made in shifting its electricity generation from coal to natural gas. By 2020, the report projects that Canada will fall well short of its stated emission-reduction targets.

China

China hasn't made any pledges to reduce its carbon emissions. As its economy grows, emissions will increase. But China has promised to become at least 40 percent more energy efficient by 2015.

China is the world's biggest producer and consumer of coal—and the No. 1 emitter of greenhouse gases and the second-largest consumer of energy. But it's also a developing nation—which means that, like other developing nations, it isn't required to lower its emissions under the Kyoto Protocol.

Still, China's coal resources aren't infinite, and as the country finds itself importing more of the fossil fuel to power its growth, it is also aggressively pursuing renewable energy sources. Chinese leaders have said they want non-fossil fuels to account for 15 percent of the nation's energy sources by 2020. Under a law passed in 2005, Chinese power grid companies are required to purchase a certain percentage of their total power supply from renewable energy sources. And China provides extensive subsidies to its clean energy sector—like the U.S., it hopes that green tech jobs can fuel future growth. Even so, many analysts warn that weaning China off coal won't be easy.

The country has also committed to boosting its forest cover, and it is experimenting with a carbon trading plan: Lawmakers recently approved a pilot program in seven provinces and cities.

European Union

The EU and its 27 member states have pledged to reduce emissions by **20 percent below 1990 levels by 2020**. *The EU has said it would bump this commitment up to 30 percent if other developed countries sign up for similar commitments.*

Under the Kyoto Protocol, the then-15 EU member states signed on to reduce emissions by 8 percent below 1990 levels by 2012. To meet that goal, in 2005 the EU launched the biggest carbon trading market in the world. Today, all 27 member states are required to participate, plus Iceland, Liechtenstein and Norway. Major factories and power plants in the EU are granted permits for how much carbon they can emit. Companies that emit less carbon than their allotted amount can sell their extra carbon credits to firms that exceed their emissions limit.

Starting in January, all airlines with flights that take off or land in Europe will be required to buy carbon permits to offset emissions from their flights. That requirement has sparked objections and legal challenges from several nations that argue it violates international law.

India

India, like China, also **won't commit to reducing its carbon emissions**—*saying that would hurt efforts to bring millions of its citizens out of poverty. But it has agreed to increase its energy efficiency by 20 percent by 2015.*

India is the world's No. 3 emitter of greenhouse gases, but because it's a developing nation, it isn't required to cut emissions under the Kyoto Protocol. That said, India is an active participant in the Clean Development Mechanism—a carbon offset plan set up under the Kyoto Protocol. Basically, the CDM lets developing nations like India earn credits for implementing emission-reducing projects. India can then sell those credits to an industrialized nation, which can count them toward its overall emissions-reduction commitment. India has hundreds of CDM projects; almost half of them focus on wind power and biomass.

India has set an ambitious goal of getting 20 gigawatts of solar power online by 2022. A gigawatt of electricity is enough to power a small city. In 2010, the country started levying a carbon tax on coal to help subsidize renewable energy projects.

Indonesia

Indonesia has pledged to cut emissions by **26 percent by 2020 from today's levels.**

Indonesia is home to vast swaths of tropical forests, which suck up atmospheric carbon. But those forests are being logged at an alarming rate—and that's releasing huge amounts of carbon into the atmosphere. Under a deal with Norway that went into effect in May 2011, Indonesia agreed to implement a two-year moratorium on new concessions for clearing forests in exchange for $1 billion in support for its forest conservation efforts.

But many observers question Indonesia's commitment to preventing deforestation, given that the country's current economic boom has been largely fueled by extraction of its natural resources.

Allegations that Forestry Ministry officials have lined their political war chests with funds raised by selling off logging rights haven't done much to bolster confidence.

Japan

*Japan has pledged to reduce its emissions by **25 percent below 1990 levels by 2020.***

The world's No. 5 greenhouse gas producer, Japan committed to reducing its emissions by 6 percent below their 1990 levels under the Kyoto Protocol, and it was largely on track to meet that goal. In 2010, it launched a cap-and-trade plan aimed at forcing some 1,300 major businesses—including large office buildings, public buildings and schools—in the Tokyo metropolitan region to reduce their emissions.

However, the Fukushima nuclear disaster threw Japan a fastball. The nation relied on nuclear power for about a third of its electricity, but in the wake of the March 2011 accident, the vast majority of its reactors have gone offline. The lost output forced Japan to institute energy-reducing measures and, in the short term, to rely more heavily on fossil fuel-burning power utilities—which boosted its emissions in 2011. With the Japanese public now wary about nuclear energy, the nation's leaders are trying to find a new way forward.

Russia

*Russia has pledged to reduce its emissions by at least **15 percent from 1990 levels**—a year when the Soviet Union was still in existence, and emissions from heavy industry, mostly related to the military, were sky high.*

When Russia ratified the Kyoto Protocol in 2004, it pledged to hold its greenhouse gas emissions at or below 1990 levels. After the Soviet Union collapsed, Russia's emissions did, too. So the country hasn't had to do much to meet its Kyoto pledges.

Indeed, Russia has long been known as a country with little regard for environmental concerns, and it is still largely dependent on many heavy industries that are considered major polluters. Despite Russian ratification of the climate pact, for a long time the country's leaders continued to question the human role in climate change.

In 2009, the Russian government quietly reversed that position, adopting a new climate doctrine that seemed to accept human contribution to global warming. The same year, the country pledged to reduce its emissions by at least 15 percent from 1990. However, this pledge still doesn't require any action on Russia's part: By some estimates, the country's emissions remain more than 30 percent below 1990 highs. Though Russia has unveiled energy-efficiency goals, analysts call the country's climate policies "a black hole."

South Africa

South Africa expects its **emissions to peak between 2020 and 2025,** *then remain flat for a decade before dropping off. By 2020, South Africa aims for emissions to top out at levels 34 percent lower than if the country were to take no actions.*

South Africa is highly dependent on coal—about 90 percent of its electricity comes from burning the fossil fuel—and it's a major contributor to greenhouse gas emissions in Africa. The nation is slowly studying cleaner energy options and more energy-efficient alternatives. But to move forward with any emission reductions, South Africa says it's going to need funding and support from industrialized nations.

South Africa's renewable energy initiative aims to make clean power account for nearly 9 percent of the nation's energy mix by 2030. But that project is just getting off the ground: Construction on the first few dozen projects, mostly wind and solar power plants, won't begin until after mid-2012 at the earliest.

The country says it's committed to making nuclear power—which currently supplies about 5 percent of its electricity—a much bigger part of its energy mix in the future. But a shortage of funding may delay those plans.

United States

*The U.S. pledged to **reduce emissions by 17 percent by 2020**, but that promise was contingent on Congress passing an aggressive cap-and-trade bill. Instead, the bill ended up in the trash, and **the U.S. hasn't made it clear how it will meet its emission goals.***

The U.S. has taken some actions at the federal level to curb emissions, including new nationwide fuel-efficiency standards for cars and light trucks. Individual states also have laws designed to lower their emissions in the coming decades. California has the most ambitious plan: Starting in 2013, the state will cap greenhouse gas emissions from factories and power plants, and, eventually, emissions from vehicles.

But even with all those state and federal actions taken together, the World Resources Institute figures that the U.S. can't achieve a 17 percent reduction in emissions by 2020. New federal laws—for example, one that puts a tax on carbon emissions—would need to fill the gap, and prospects for that aren't good.

Sustainable Development Can Combat Global Disaster

Tom R. Burns and Nora Machado Des Johansson

In this viewpoint, the authors, who are both researchers associated with Portugal's Centre for Research in Sociology at the University Institute of Lisbon, consider how sustainability and sustainable development relate to disaster risk reduction and climate change adaptation. They explore sustainability from a social systemic perspective—encompassing the various functionalities of a social system and the interrelationships in specific environmental contexts.

As you read, consider the following questions:

1. What did the UN World Commission on Environment and Development hope to accomplish with its report?
2. What can we learn from the examples of Gotland and Sweden?
3. What is the benefit of sustainable development to the fight against climate change?

1. Sustainability and Sustainable Development

Sustainability: Background and Definition

The literature on the concepts "sustainability" and "sustainable development" is vast [1]. These influential concepts emerged out of political and administrative processes, not scientific ones. Like the concept of development itself, sustainable development has been a contentious and contested concept, not only with respect to controversies between advocates of capitalism and those of socialism and social democracy, but between industrialized and developed countries, or between modernization advocates and their diverse opponents. In other words, environmental issues have been added to earlier contentious issues. These have been and continue to be divisive, for instance between those who, on the one hand, advocate limiting or blocking much socio-economic development in order to protect or reclaim the environment and those who, on the other hand, stress the need of socio-economic development to alleviate poverty and inequality, if necessary at the expense of the state of the environment.

Historically, the linkage of sustainability and development has been, in large part, the result of global political and administrative processes and the diverse interests driving these processes. The term "sustainable development" was coined as a political-administrative term to bridge differences between developed and developing countries in the context of UN negotiations and resolutions. The UN World Commission on Environment and Development (hereafter, World Commission), chaired by Gro Harlam Brundtland (former Norwegian Prime Minister), produced an influential report in 1987, Our Common Future (World Commission [2]). The Brundtland Commission had been established by the UN in 1983 in response to growing awareness and concerns of the deterioration of the human environment and natural resources at the same time that developing countries were pushing for higher levels of economic growth (with the likelihood of increased damage to the environment). The Commission was to address the environmental challenge as it was intertwined with economic and social issues.

The Commission concerned itself with environment and growth/development as well as a number of related issues. The term "sustainability development" (SD) was intended to build bridges between the economic, ecological, and social areas of concern. Above all, the concept was meant to refer to development that meets the needs of the present generation without compromising (or jeopardizing) the ability of future generations to meet their needs (numerous other definitions have been proposed [1]; among others see [3,4,5,6]). It was intended to build bridges between, on the one hand, developed countries particularly concerned about issues of sustainability and, on the other hand, developing countries determined to industrialize and develop themselves economically and socially [2]. A precise definition of sustainable development, based on entirely technical or ecological criteria is not feasible; concepts such as "sustainable development" and "sustainability" are normative and political ones [5], much like "democracy," "social justice," "equality," "liberty," etc. rather than precise, scientific concepts (Sustainability and sustainable development differ in that the former refers to a complex of values/goals to be realized, while the latter refers to the process of societal change aiming at, and moving toward, sustainability goals).

As normative concepts, they are contested and part of struggles over the direction and speed of social, economic, and political initiatives and developments in the global context [7,8]. Similarly, DRR and CCA are also normative concepts This means that—unlike purely scientific concepts such as force, electric charge, negative feedback, complex social network—they provide policy orientation and a normative or moral "force" (Disaster risk reduction (DRR) is defined by UNISDR as the systematic development and application of policies, strategies, institutional arrangements, and practices to minimize vulnerabilities, hazards, and the unfolding of disaster impacts throughout a society [9]; Climate Change Adaptation (CCA) is defined by the IPCC as "adjustment in natural or human systems in response to actual or expected climatic developments or their effects, so as to moderate harm or to exploit beneficial opportunities" [10]).

Sustainability, as a normative and political concept, is used, among other things, to refer to a fair distribution of natural resources among populations of the world today as well as among different generations over time. It concerns also values and "rights" to existence of other species as well as notions about how much environmental capital one generation should bequeath to the next [5]. In the language of policymaking, reference is often made to the three or more pillars or fields of sustainable development: effective and enduring normatively satisfying economic functioning and prosperity, social welfare and justice, political deliberation and decision-making, and environmental protection. The most difficult challenge is to determine how one combines and balances these in a sustainable manner, particularly since under many conditions they are contradictory: economic growth may be accomplished at the cost of environmental protection and conservation, or economic growth is sacrificed for the sake of increased public welfare and distributive justice.

The concept's power and also contentiousness relates to it bringing together these apparently contradictory environmental, economic, social and political imperatives. Harris [11] emphasizes that its contestation arises not only from the emphasis placed on diverse imperatives but from the difficulties encountered in their practical combination and realization.

The sustainability perspective calls for a complex systems model of society and the latter's multiple interactions with its physical and social environment [1]. In part, this is because sustainable development focuses our attention on multi-functionality and multiple-dimensional interactions.

2. Social System Model

Drawing on earlier work [1,12,13], our point of departure is a model of complex systems (ecological as well as social) with which to characterize and analyze DRR, CCA, and SD, all of which are instances of complex systems. The model is based on a social science theory of dynamic, complex systems [12,13,14,15,16]. After introducing the theory here, we apply it in formulating models applicable to complex, multi-faceted, dynamic systems: socio-technical systems such as adaptation subsystems and disaster reduction subsystems. Such systems are not only multi-dimensional but typically have multiple vulnerabilities to diverse hazards internally or externally generated [17]. The systems are subject to perturbation/change—due to external forces or internal processes. Their responses are usually non-linear, and not fully predictable (in part because there are unintended and unanticipated impacts), and, therefore, also not fully controllable.

Consider a complex social system with a population of social actors, rule regime(s) underlying social relationships and interaction patterns, resources (materials and technologies), multiple production processes functioning in their social and ecological contexts:

(1) Our perspective entails the following dynamics patterns: Complex "social systems" have multiple subsystems with multiple interrelated functionalities (economic, socio-cultural, educational, political, etc.). In complex systems a number of DRR subsystems as well as CCA subsystems are likely to be included designed to deal with particular stressors, for example, earthquakes, floods, spread of dangerous diseases (or their vectors). DRR and CAA stressors are addressed by one or several selected subsystems (in many cases, they may be largely local in character).

(2) Functioning systems are subject to external and internal stresses of varying degrees of hazard. Some stressors may result in systemic performance failings, possibly disasters. That is, failure to avoid some hazardous stressors or to regulate/control/block

them results in malfunctioning and even substantial damage to the system, the people involved, the property, and essential resources, in short, systemic disaster.

(3) Our systems approach views agents as acting within (embedded in) and also upon systems (performing in them as well as adapting and transforming them through multi-level governance arrangements). Agents in any given system (and also possibly external agents) make judgments about adaptation and risk reduction measures as well as sustainability measures. They assess performances, risks, hazards, vulnerabilities, adaptation and sustainability needs. This entails normatively oriented judgment and risk logic(s).

(4) Responses to stressor are typically in the form of built-in algorithms and procedures that are activated as well as agent-responses (through monitoring, innovating, taking actions to regulate, ban, or avoid the stressors). Multiple agents are typically involved, managers, experts, operatives who make use of appropriate materials and technologies, and operate according to a design.

The systemic model enables a robust conception of sustainability and sustainable development. As we have seen, it identifies hazards and opportunities for DRR and CCA as well as risk reduction for other challenges. DRR (and CCA as well as other systems or subsystems) entail constructions (or re-constructions) of subsystems for the purpose of response to stressors and involve such operations as "avoiding, regulating/blocking, reducing vulnerability, transforming the stressors and/or the social system as a whole.

The concerns here include restructuring or transforming a given system in order to adapt to or to overcome stressors such as climate change or other global environmental change (GEC), reducing exposure to hazards, reducing vulnerability, reducing or repairing damages to the system or system components effectively. System adaptation/transition may accomplish then a reduction in a stressor or vulnerability to it. A systems perspective enables us to identify social structural, political, and agential factors relating to system stressors such as destruction of infrastructure, weather changes, new disease vectors, and other vulnerabilities to them— and how major agents in a system respond to these with strategies to overcome—or perhaps fail in their efforts. In particular:

- Multiple powerful agents—those controlling essential resources and expertise in the system—must be mobilized and coordinated to address the hazards and vulnerabilities (and to overcome barriers and opposition to adaptation and systemic transition).

- That is, mobilizing and coordinating agents gain access to essential resources, authorities experts, stakeholders, etc. to address system stressors.

- There are typically multiple adaptations to one or more stressors: for instance, in the case of climate change, flood control response may be combined with retrofitting buildings to be more robust or less vulnerable to moisture and mildew.

Thus, we emphasize not only the importance of agents—and their culture, capabilities, and access to resources—but also the complex social systems in which agents interact and upon which they operate. A complex social system has populations of social actors, rule regimes of social and cultural structures, resources (materials and technologies), and multiple production processes in a social and ecological context.

The systems model enables us to systemically describe and analyze such constructed subsystems as those of DRR and CCA (Section 3). These subsystem constructions were launched and developed by agents in order to deal with climate change and other system challengers. But many system functions do not relate directly to climate change or DRR. Sustainable development entails a global perspective that encompasses multiple subsystems, which are differentiated and have diverse functionalities.

3. Case Studies of Response to Stressors

For our purposes here we consider two types of stressors (which may overlap): disaster with the action of DRR and the hazard influencer of climate change with the action of CCA—that is, actors' responses to these. Section 3.1 presents two DRR cases, one concerning food security, the other concerning chemical security. The cases are based on EU policy research; the methods were multiple: interviews with informants and experts, documents and research materials, and reports in the mass media. Section 3.2 presents CCA cases, one about the island of Gotland, Sweden, the other about the Gothenburg Metropolitan Area (GMA). Both of these cases are based on analyses of official documents, research reports, and mass media coverage as well as personal experience and observation (living on Gotland and in Gothenburg).

3.1. DRR

Reducing exposure to hazards, lessening vulnerability of people and property, effective management of land and the environment, and improving preparedness for adverse events are all examples of disaster risk reduction [18,19]. Natural and man-made hazards—and societal vulnerabilities to these—are reduced through proper disaster management policy, material and institutional development policies and constructions. As a result of failures to introduce or maintain disaster management policy and practices, disaster risk and disaster losses are likely to increase in the case of hazardous systems [17].

Highly risky disaster systems (whether due to technologies, the complexity of socio-technical systems, ecological contexts, or the participating agents) are those which have the potential (a certain (even if very low) likelihood, to cause great harm to property and people involved, partners or clients, third parties, other species, and the environment. Some risky systems have catastrophic potential in that they are capable in case of a performance or regulatory failure to kill hundreds or thousands, wiping out species, or irreversibly contaminating the atmosphere, water, and land.

DRRs make up systems, typically complex, with particular measures or operations to reduce risks from external stressors and/or internal stressors (through monitoring, testing, and actions to ban or regulate); multiple agents are involved, managers, experts, operatives, and use is made of appropriate materials and technologies, operating according to a design. There are production processes, governance and regulative processes within the system and also externally. Examples are nuclear power facilities, flight control systems, chemical regulatory systems, food regulatory systems, renewable energy sources which may contribute to, for instance, sustainability and climate change adaptation but entail new risks, or limit new forms of CCA and DRR: thus, tigers/wolves and other predators which contribute to biodiversity may increase risks of "accidents" with livestock and children; policies and programs to reduce hazards of and adapt to climate change challenges may increase risks of economic and political threats.

Two significant instances of DRR, which we have investigated, relate to EU policymaking and regulation regarding food and chemical safety. Although these are both large sectors with multiple stressors and disaster risks, they cover only narrow fields of societal stressors and vulnerabilities.

[…]

3.2. CCA

Climate change is characterized by, among other things, uncertainty about its future trajectory, its phases and timing and about potential impacts and non-containability within existing borders of jurisdiction [22]. Examples of climate change stressors are changed rain intensities, altered precipitation patterns such as clustering or longer rain duration, runoff following snowmelt in combination with rain.

Examples of climate change adaptation are the introduction or development of infrastructures to reduce associated peak flows and flooding consequences in a given environment, development of new designs for built environments against moisture and flooding, development of more effective urban drainage systems, particularly as on the Swedish West Coast (Gothenburg and Malmo) where higher sea levels are likely to be combined with heavier rainfalls resulting in flooding of coastal and low land areas, with likely damage to infrastructures and buildings as well as threat to human life.

In general, key agents in social systems "adapt" (withdraw or change behavior/habitat) to prevent or avoid certain hazards, disasters (losses, damages), among others, climate change stressors. Even DRR is a form of "adaptation to,"

- Disappearance of or threat to the group's/community's island or coast, and, construction of walls

- Retrofit house because of more extreme weather, increase of rain and moisture in the area

- Educate and vaccinate in response to new disease vectors (ticks, mosquitoes carrying malaria...) emerge and adapt by educating people about the threat, precautions to take, and conducting campaigns.

Many disasters from climate change can be prevented. Buildings can be constructed to effectively survive increased humidity and flooding. Infrastructures (dams, canals, causeways, other barriers) can be constructed and integrated with ecosystems to limit flooding and erosion.

On many vulnerable coasts—where coastal erosion is occurring—those living there construct barriers against flooding and erosion. In Sweden, for instance, the threat of extreme rainfall and low land flooding has led to the development of methods to reduce or regulate peak flows and flooding consequences: (1) retreat (this means moving populations (human and animals) and infrastructure and other built environments, e.g., movement to safer grounds; (2) defend (defending against the stressors, e.g., to protect an urban area or lowland through flood defense, e.g., a wall (reducing levels of risk combined with cost minimization); (3) proactive response to, for example, rising sea levels through new construction in locations expected to be secure.

In many parts of the world, substantial floods occur regularly for millions of people who live in the low-lying riverine islands and coastlines. When floods occur, households often flee, if relevant giving their cattle to friends and neighbors to look after while they recover from flooding. In many coastal regions people use concrete blocks and trees such as mangrove trees to provide simple erosion protection and stilt houses to reduce flooding risks. In dry or semi-arid region, withdrawal is also a common response. For instance, water is critical in Tahova, a dry land region of Niger. Crops are difficult to grow in the dry season, so men migrate to the cities for work. Historically, water has also been stored or channeled from distant areas.

Case 1: Gotland, Sweden Responding to Climate Change
The Baltic island of Gotland is expected to be (and has already found itself becoming) subject to significant CC stressors, above all higher levels of precipitation and its multiple impacts as well as new disease vectors and diseases [23]. Reponses have been disease campaigns (including vaccination) to deal with the spread through ticks of borrelia and tick-borne encephalitis (TBE) and retrofit of buildings to deal with greater moisture (and coastal erosion). Planning and educational programs have been established. The significance of climate change for the island is widely recognized at the local (municipal), regional (Gotland region), and national levels. Like Gothenburg it is trying to move beyond the thinking of climate change adaptation and to envision a "sustainable Gotland" by promoting green (renewable) energy (already there are 170 windmills producing 380 gwk meeting 40% of the island electricity needs); the Island has an integrated recycling system which, among other things, produces biogas for public transportation; a desalination plant is being constructed; new kinds of nature tourism is being developed (tourism is a major economic sector on Gotland along with agriculture); there are restrictions on new building construction in coastal areas at heights under 2 m over sea level; much attention is being given research

and education because of major gaps in knowledge and policy experience confronting Gotland today.

Responses to climate change can vary greatly, depending on conceptual models, material resources, leadership, institutions and culture. The large (for Sweden) metropolitan area of Gothenburg suggests some of this and also points up that Gothenburg, like Gotland, is increasingly thinking in terms of sustainability rather than climate change adaptation and disaster risk reduction.

CASE: Gothenburg Metropolitan Area [22]
Climate change in the Gothenburg area threatens with increased flooding, slides, erosion, new diseases and disease vectors. Gothenburg Metropolitan area (GMA)—expected to be the part of Sweden most affected by the impacts of climate change—is addressing and acting upon relevant issues of climate change adaptation. This has been done within the framework of Sweden's Planning and Building Act which puts responsibility with local governments for dealing in the "common interest" of climate adaptation.

Gothenburg has developed a perspective and strategy for an environmental (and sustainable development) program as opposed to a purely climate program. The city stresses that climate work needs to be coordinated and guided toward long-term sustainability; climate need to be considered in the context of multiple environmental challenges and the measures to deal with them.

The stress then is on a broad systemic approach extending across multiple societal areas essential to sustainability: energy, transport, water supply regulation, building and infrastructure, education, consumption, social planning.

To encompass the totality of the challenge:

• "sustainable Gothenburg" has become a key normative public concept.

• A concept of sustainability relevant to the city, the "3-river city," has been developed. Among other things, this entails changing standards of expected flood levels and developing plans and programs to deal with expected impacts such as flooding, slides/erosion and loss or contamination of freshwater supply. In restructuring waterways and building barriers, there is both climate change adaptation and disaster risk reduction; regulating the water levels of the 3 major rivers is also both CCA and DRR.

- A green construction programme involves designating locations of building (LAFE) safe from flooding and slides for the purpose of authorizing building permits. The island Tjorn recommended a LAFE above the average sea water level for all buildings and infrastructures with vital societal functions and for all new buildings and transport lanes. Several municipal masterplans require geotechnical stability investigations relating to slides and erosion as precondition for detail planning and building permits.

- There is ongoing construction, operation, and maintenance of infrastructure to reduce climate and environmental impacts.

- Gothenburg has been orienting itself to sustainability-conscious consumption including climate conscious consumption (and to reduce climate impact of food production and transportation). This entails, among other things, reducing the purchase of resource-intensive goods.

- Waste is to be reduced and the current high level of recycling developed further.

- Conducting research on issues, strategies, and consequences of sustainability and climate change adaptations, for instance, economic analyses of the costs (damages) from climate change versus the costs of measures to adapt and to prepare.

4. Sustainable Development as a Societal Development System

4.1. CCA and DRR Are Only Partial Systems

Sustainability judgments, designs, institutional arrangements, and developments would optimally include (or embed), among other things, appropriate and satisfactory CCA as well as appropriate and satisfactory DRR. System sustainability is multi-dimensional and with defined standards that surpass "sufficient adaptation" or "sufficient disaster risk reduction." As suggested above, the latter are only partial. In contrast to sustainable development arrangements where multiple functionalities and the interrelationships of multiple "pillars" are built in conceptually and practically, CCA and DRR models tend to leave out or leave implicit a number of key functionalities, for instance, agential aspects (training and education, the necessary professionalism), reliable appropriate materials and technologies, and the sustained over time budgeting (private and/public). These factors must be included in a broad or systemic perspective, as in sustainability models, in ways that are not inherent to DRR or CCA subsystems. Pelling [24] also stresses such limitations of CCA and the need to take into account political, institutional, cultural, and ecological factors; see also [25].

In the conceptualization of CCA and DRR, in contrast to sustainability's multi-functionality conception, that typically take as a point of departure sustained budgeting levels, the support and legitimation of key societal actors, and the education of experts to manage and operate disaster risk reduction apparatuses—that is, the economic, socio-cultural, and political bases for financing and operating the systems. In a sustainability perspective these are taken into account explicitly.

The argument here suggests that CCA and DRR arrangements may or may not be sustainable over the medium-to-long-run. This may be for economic reasons, ecological/natural resource constraints, or socio-cultural forces (refusal of the population to sufficiently change life-style or make necessary institutional and economic changes (replacing fossil fuels with renewable energy sources and controlling pollution and environmental degradation, among others).

Although CCA and DRR are only partial systems, they may relate to one another in systemic terms [26,27]. But they are not necessarily compatible with sustainable development, as we now discuss.

4.2. Possible Incompatibility of CCA and DRR Systems with Overall Social System Sustainability

As suggested above, DRR and CCA may not be compatible with sustainable development, in that their scope may be far-too-narrow, ignoring a number of key dimensions of sustainable development in the social systemic context such as increased reliance on renewable energy, biodiversity support, and chemical pollution reduction. At the same time, policymaking agents may accept disaster risks (and reject adapting to climate change or other threats because of lack of resources, or poor judgment of cost/benefit imbalances or priorities elsewhere).

Or, as pointed out below, it may be a matter of prioritization or practices of risk-taking. In responding to stressor(s), agents may prioritize broad sustainability over particular disaster risks including those influenced by climate change, like sacrificing a leg for survival of the rest of the body. Or vice versa, one may risk the social system as a whole to save an important part of the system; for instance, the system's elite or its particular social structure (e.g., an apartheid system). Or, for the sake of technological advancement, one takes unknown risks with Genetically Modified Organisms in the context of 100% sustainable food supply. In these cases, CCA could be said to trump sustainability from the perspective of a high risk-taker. Thus, one may succeed in accomplishing DRR and CCA without achieving or maintaining medium-to-long-run sustainability. Consequently, successful DRR (possibly involving CCA, or not) may accomplish (immediate objective(s)) but may be unsustainable over time or over an extended space—in short, they are unsustainable subsystems. Unsustainability may be caused by (1) insufficient resources (including technologies); (2) agents' insufficient knowledge and/or capabilities; (3) insufficient coordination and effective governance (organizational); (4) insufficient socio-political legitimacy and political support.

4.3. DRR and CCA Should Be Subjected to Sustainability Standards, Discourses, and Judgments

The DRR and CCA subsystems are judged to be sustainable if and only if (1) essential inputs into these subsystems are sustainable (or replaceable with sustainable factors when used up); (2) subsystem outputs do not undermine, block, or interfere with the sustainability of other subsystems or with the social system as a whole. That is, a given subsystem in its interactions with other subsystems may produce disaster risks (or increases in disaster risks) or produce developments that undermine, block, or interfere with sustainability conditions and mechanisms.

In general, from a holistic, societal perspective, DRR and CCA can be viewed and assessed in relation to the societal multi-functionality and long time scale of sustainable development. Sustainability incorporates capacities to deal with such potential systemic disturbances as climate change (as well as other hazardous global changes), either through prevention or avoidance and/or adaptation.

Several key points in this part are: (1) One may accomplish disaster risk reduction which in the medium to long run is not sustainable in terms of ecological, economic, or socio-political dimensions; (2) One may also have adaptation with respect to a stressor X, for instance climate change, without system or even subsystem sustainability; (3) DRR and CCA may be pursued separately or pursued as part of an overall initiative to adapt to particular climate change impacts in such a way as to reduce disaster risk; (4) DRR and CCA—while important sources of conceptual and methodological tools—may lead to non-sustainable judgments and developments. In other words, improvements in DRR and CCA may not be sustainable over the long run because of their unintended or unanticipated impacts on key sustainability dimensions; (5) Note that the systems model alerts us and enables us to analytically differentiate DRR, CCA, and sustainability development. It is argued here that DRR and CCA should and can be related to the medium term- long-term goals of sustainable development; (6) In general, the factor of sustainability trumps DRR and CCA in terms of impact assessment and design, but there are other considerations as discussed below.

4.4. Distinctions Between Sustainable and Non-Sustainable DRR and CCA

DRR for a particular hazard (e.g., volcanic eruption, earthquake, soil erosion, salination of the soil) may or may not be sustainable in the long-run. It may be unsustainable because, for instance:

- The DRR action or its socio-technical system makes use of non-renewable, non-replaceable resources

- Or the DRR system blocks necessary adaptation of the more encompassing social system, for instance by draining away resources essential to the sustainability of the larger system. As a result of this systemic non-sustainability, the DRR sub-system will fail to be maintained over the medium to long run.

- In the prevailing socio-cultural and economic perspective, people are unwilling to make the sacrifices for DRR, for instance, they are willing to accept the risk of a volcano or earthquake, or the rising seas.

In sum, sustainability developments, judgments, designs, and institutional arrangements may include (or embed), among other things, appropriate and satisfactory CCA placed within appropriate and satisfactory DRR. System sustainability is multi-dimensional and with defined limits that surpass "sufficient adaptation" or sufficient DRR. The latter are only partial.

On the other hand, a "necessary" CCA or DRR infrastructure may or may not be sustainable over the medium to long-run.

This may be for economic reasons, ecological/natural resource constraints, or socio-cultural forces (refusal of the population to sufficiently change life-style or to make necessary institutional and economic changes (for instance, shifting from fossil fuels to renewable energy sources).

5. Concluding Remarks

The sustainability or sustainable development perspective provides a systemic view, indicating the complex interdependencies among essential subsystems to human welfare and survival. Societal sectors or specialized subsystems like DRR or the CCA subsystem within it are insufficiently comprehensive when viewed from the perspective of a sustainability framework; they do not explicitly take into account the systemic economic, socio-cultural, and political factors in societal survival and even the question of the availability of long-term resources for CCA and DRR subsystems themselves (long-term resource availability and sufficient prioritization of the resources in competition with other demands).

The conception of sustainable development orients us not only to ecological factors and the interaction of the ecological, and the social. It also orients us to the economic conditions and processes, the essential conditions for financing and maintaining subsystems or programs of DRR as well as CCA; and it orients us to consider socio-cultural conditions essential to policy legitimation and the maintenance of societal support and a readiness to aim for wider sustainability. Sustainable development is concerned about social systems as a whole and the long-time scale. A complex systems perspective encompasses then not just functionality and simple cost-benefit issues but multi-functional and multi-dimensional sustainability: it considers that a sub-system may contribute not only to ecological sustainability but to the economy, to cooperation and coordination, and other governance mechanisms as well as legitimacy socio-cultural integration, and political order.

And, as we have seen, a system may be sustainable and include its climate change adaptability (as well as perhaps other environmental change adaptability) within its DRR capacity as well as DRR capacity beyond CCA. But, as indicated in Section 4, the designs, realizations and practices of CCA and DRR subsystems should be incorporated into a sustainable development model, its standards and values, discourses, plans, and institutional arrangements. Failure to do this would mean, in general, that DRR subsystems and CCA—and the social system in which they are embedded—may not be sustainable or only precariously sustainable (because vulnerable to particular internal and/or external stressors). Thus, as discussed earlier in the chapter, a well-functioning DRR subsystem or a well-functioning CCA subsystem may be non-sustainable for long-term economic reasons, or for socio-cultural or political reasons; or indirectly, the DRR or CCA subsystem drains away essential resources or interferes with key systemic mechanisms essential to global system sustainability.

Part of sustainable development discourses entail exploring alternative DRR subsystems as well as alternative CCA subsystems, namely finding or developing DRR or CCA subsystems that are more likely to be sustainable. They would be designed and assessed so as to take into account economic, socio-cultural, and political dimensions, thereby increasing systemic chances of medium to long-term sustainability.

References and Notes

1. Burns, T.R. Sustainable development: Agents, systems and the environment. *Curr. Sociol.* 2016, *64*, 875–906.
2. World Commission on Environment and Development. *Our Common Future*; Oxford University Press: London, UK, 1987.
3. Drummond, I.; Marsden, T. *Sustainable Development: The Impasse and beyond from the Condition of Sustainability*; Routledge: London, UK, 1999.
4. Goodland, R. The concept of sustainable development. *Annu. Rev. Ecol. Syst.* 1995, *26*, 1–24.
5. Opschoor, J.; van der Straaten, J. Sustainable development: An institutional approach. *Ecol. Econ.* 1993, *7*, 203–222. Available online: www.geocities.ws /saxifraga_2000/costanza.doc (accessed on 10 December 2016).
6. WWF Global. *Living Planet Report 2002*; WWF International: Gland, Switzerland, 1996.
7. Baker, S. The Evolution of EU Environmental Policy: From Growth to Sustainable Development. In *The Politics of Sustainable Development: Theory, Policy and Practice*

within the European Union; Baker, S., Kousis, M., Richardson, D., Young, S.C., Eds.; Routledge: London, UK, 1996.

8. Lafferty, W.M. The implementation of sustainable development in the European Union. In *Contemporary Political Studies*; Lovenduski, J., Stanyer, J., Eds.; PSA: Belfast, Northern Ireland, 1995.

9. UNISDR. *Living with Risk: A Global Review of Disaster Reduction Initatives, Terminology on Disaster Risk Reduction*; UNISDR: Geneva, Switzerland, 2004.

10. McCarthy, J.J.; Lanziani, O.F.; Leary, N.A.; Dokken, D.J.; White, K.S. *IPCC Climate Change 2001: Impacts, Adaptation, and Vulnerabillity*; Cambridge University Press: Cambridge, UK, 2001.

11. Harris, J.M. Basic principles of sustainable development. In *The Encyclopedia of Life Support Systems*; UNESCO: Paris, France, 2001.

12. Burns, T.R. The Sociology of Complex Systems: An Overview of Actor-Systems-Dynamics. *World Futures J. Gen. Evol.* 2006, *62*, 411–460.

13. Burns, T.R.; Baumgartner, T.; DeVille, P. *Man, Decision and Society*; Gordon and Breach: London, UK, 1985.

14. Burns, T.R. System Theories. In *The Blackwell Encyclopedia of Sociology*; Blackwell Publishing: Oxford, UK, 2006.

15. Baumgartner, T.; Burns, T.R.; DeVille, P. *The Shaping of Socio-economic; Systems: The Application of the Theory of Actor-System Dynamics to Conflict, Social Power, and Economic Innovation in Economic Life*; Routledge: London, UK, 2014.

16. Burns, T.R.; Hall, P. *The Meta-power Paradigm: Causalities, Mechanisms, & Constructions*; Peter Lang: Frankfurt, Germany; Berlin, Germany; Oxford, UK, 2012.

17. Burns, T.R.; Machado, N. Technology, Complexity, and Risk: Part I: Social Systems Analysis of Risky Sociotechnical Systems and the Likelihood of Accidents. 2009. Available online: http://uu.diva-portal.org/smash/get/diva2:685825/FULLTEXT01 .pdf (accessed on 15 February 2017).

18. UNISDR. *Terminology on Disaster Risk Reduction*; UNISDR: Geneva, Switzerland, 2009.

19. Smith, K.; Petley, D.N. *Mass Movement Hazards Environmental Hazards Assessing Risk and Reducing Disaster*; MPG Books Ltd.: Bodmin, UK; Routledge: London, UK, 2009.

20. Carson, M.; Burns, T.R.; Calvo, D. *Public Policy Paradigms: Theory and Practice of Paradigms Shifts in the EU*; Peter Lang: Frankfurt, Germany; Berlin, Germany; Oxford, UK, 2009.

21. Carson, R. *The Silent Spring*; Houghton Mifflin: Boston, MA, USA, 1962.

22. Lundqvist, L. Planning for Climate Change Adaptation in a Multi-level Context: The Gothenburg Metropolitan Area. *Eur. Plan. Stud.* 2016, *24*, 1–20.

23. Thörn, P.; Bonnier, E.; Roth, S. *Klimatanpassning* (Climate Adaptation) 2016—*Så långt har Sveriges Kommuner Kommit*. 2016. Available online: http://www.ivl.se /download/18.29aef808155c0d7f0504f1/1472806321253/B2261.pdf (accessed on 10 December 2016).

24. Pelling, M. *Adaptation to Climate Change: From Resilence to Transformation*; Routledge: London, UK, 2011.

25. Blaikie, P.; Cannon, T.; Davis, I.; Wisner, B. *At Risk: Natural Hazards, People's Vulnerability, and Disasters*, 2nd ed.; Routledge: New York, NY, USA, 2004.

26. Kelman, I.; Gaillard, J.C. Embedding Climate Change Adaptation within Disaster Risk Reduction. In *Climate Change Adaptation and Disaster Risk Reduction: Issues and Challenges*; Shaw, R., Pulhin, J.M., Pereira, J.J., Eds.; Emerald: Bingley, UK, 2010; pp. 23–46.

27. They overlap. CCA relates to DRR [23] in the sense that climate change may engender disaster risks such as rising sea waters submerging low-lying islands or new disease vectors emerging to threaten populations of people and animals (for instance, the substantial change in weather conditions and expansion of ticks in the Baltic islands as temperatures rise and local climate conditions change). An appropriate CCA system under these conditions would include DRR components and mechanisms, that is, the DRRs are responses to climate change threats-of-disaster. But, obviously, many cases of DRR don't relate to climate change, and many climate changes don't entail disaster threats although they may be disruptive or aggravating.

Preventing Further Climate Upheaval Isn't Just the Government's Domain

Bonizella Biagini and Alan Miller

In the following viewpoint, Bonizella Biagini, who currently manages the UNDP's Programme on Climate Information for Resilient Development in Africa, and Alan Miller discuss the importance of involving the private sector—meaning non-governmental businesses and organizations—in helping developing countries cope with climate change and why these efforts might be difficult.

As you read, consider the following questions:

1. What group is experiencing a disproportionate impact from climate change?
2. What is one reason why the private sector should be involved in climate change efforts in developing countries?
3. How can businesses overcome barriers to helping developing countries?

Introduction

With the growing expectation of more rapid increases in global temperature and predictions of more frequent and severe extreme weather events, there is an urgent need to engage the private sector in efforts to improve adaptation to climate change. Climate change is already disproportionately impacting the economically disadvantaged and slowing development (WB WDR, 2010), a disparity which is likely to increase as global warming exceeds tolerable levels and climate change accelerates. In the industrialized countries, extreme weather events are already a business risk, and awareness of climate change appears to be increasing. In contrast, in developing countries, engaging the business community has been given much less emphasis and remains unusual. The authors aim to bring empirical data and operational experience to the often theoretical discussion of adaptation, based on direct experience in managing concrete adaptation projects in developing countries, through several adaptation funds, including the Least Developed Countries Fund (LDCF), the Special Climate change Fund (SCCF), the Adaptation Fund (AF) and Pilot Program on Climate Resilience (PPCR). For this purpose, this article includes an analysis of an adaptation project portfolio currently under implementation that provides some concrete examples of barriers, challenges and opportunities for private sector engagement in adaptation.

[...]

The private sector should be an active partner in and, in many instances, the dominant source of efforts to adapt to climate change. Several actions are essential for the private sector to become more fully engaged and effective in responding to climate change in developing countries. First, increase greater awareness about the significance of climate change; second, include the private sector in national and international adaptation efforts; and third, engage the private sector in developing products and services that can reduce the costs and impacts of climate change. While a general discussion of these issues is available in the literature (see, e.g., Atteridge, 2011; Schalatek &Nakhooda, 2013; Buchner et al, 2012;

and Venugopol and Srivastava, 2012), this paper promotes the specific business planning, operational practices, and new product development of the private sector that can reduce the economic and human impact of extreme weather events and other climate impacts in developing countries.

Importance of Engaging the Private Sector in Developing Country Climate Change Efforts

Engaging the private sector as a partner in recognizing and adapting to climate change in developing countries is essential for multiple reasons: to mobilize financial resources and technical capacity, leverage the efforts of governments, engage civil society and community efforts, and develop innovative climate services and adaptation technologies. Private entities dominate many decisions key to adaptation (e.g., the location and design of roads, buildings and other infrastructure investments, which are often minimally regulated by codes); agricultural research (e.g., to develop more drought-resistant seeds); water management infrastructure and technologies; the commitment of financing, much of which will necessarily have to come from private sources; the development of adaptive technologies in all development sectors; and the development and dissemination of adaptation products and services.

The private sector *should* engage in adapting to climate risks because financial impacts related to floods, droughts, hurricanes, high temperatures, and other weather related disasters have risen steadily due to climate change. (The degree to which they *will* engage depends on numerous factors which influence business decisions, as discussed below.) The number and financial consequences of extreme weather events have risen dramatically in frequency and severity in recent years with losses from weather-related events exceeding $1 trillion between 1980 and 2011 in North America alone (Munich Re, 2012). Losses from extreme weather events are increasingly a factor in corporate balance sheets as indicated by a recent review of "Physical Risks from Climate Change: A Guide for Companies and Investors on Disclosure and Management of Climate Impacts" (Ceres 2012):

- More than 160 companies in Thailand's textile industry were harmed by 2011 floods, stopping about a quarter of the country's garment production.

- Agribusiness and food company Bunge reported a $56 million quarterly loss in its sugar and bioenergy segments, driven primarily by droughts in 2010 in its main growing areas.

- Electric power company Constellation Energy experienced reduced quarterly earnings of about $0.16 per share due to the record-setting 2011 heat wave in Texas that forced it to buy incremental power at peak prices.

Insurance company Munich Re received claims worth more than $350 million from the 2010-2011 Australian floods, contributing to a 38 percent quarterly profit decline. A single extreme weather incident, such as floods in Thailand in December 2011, can reduce a country's GDP by several percent, eliminate tens of thousands of jobs, and disrupt global supply chains for manufacturing products from cars to computers (World Bank GFDRR, 2012).

The indirect effect of extreme weather events can also dramatically impact business. For example, ports may suffer from disruptions in the transport of goods due to floods even if protected themselves (IFC, 2011). A more subtle, but even more dramatic example is the connection between commercial business and extended droughts in several wheat-growing regions, resulting in shortages, a rapid rise in prices, food riots and civil unrest (Technology Review, 2011).

Private initiatives are not a substitute for governmental adaptation efforts, and indeed, the former are very dependent on the latter for information, supportive policies and regulation, and other support. Some elements of climate change adaptation are primarily or even exclusively government functions and are likely to remain so, particularly the provision of basic weather and climate information, design and implementation of risk management policies (e.g., building codes, land use restrictions, and insurance regulations), and disaster planning and preparedness.

A focus on private action has been also perceived as politically contentious insofar as seen as a means of shifting responsibility otherwise appropriately born by governments. The United Framework Convention on Climate Change (UNFCCC) includes several articles and subsequent decisions related to adaptation that assign obligations to governments. Yet, even at this early stage of implementing adaptation measures, potential private sector contributions have been identified in all these fields, and in the climate negotiations, public officials have repeatedly emphasized the importance of involving the private sector. This will be especially important in order to fulfill the financial pledges made to support the Green Climate Fund, a new financial mechanism being created as part of the decision to mobilize and channel additional funds to climate finance (Green Climate Fund websitewww.gcfund.net.)

[…]

Barriers to Increasing Private Sector Adaptation Efforts in Developing Countries

Businesses are accustomed to uncertainty in many forms, including actions by competitors, changing customer preferences, and shifts in government policies. Climate variability has long been an important uncertainty for business planning. Farmers have had to prepare for droughts and floods since biblical times. Utilities plan their operations around the hottest summer demands. Preparing for hurricanes is a fact of life in the Caribbean. The challenge in anticipating climate change arguably differs quantitatively because risks of climate change are higher as demonstrated by the higher frequency and intensity of climate related events and the economic losses that are derived from them. It also differs qualitatively because a better knowledge of the risk will allow more planned and specific prevention measures. Business planning has typically been defined by financial time horizons and spatial scales much smaller than can be obtained from current climate science and models (Connell, Miller, and Stenek, 2009). Climate change also can present qualitatively different risks from those business has faced in the past insofar as droughts, storms, and winds become much more severe than ever before.

From a private sector perspective, the perception is that while climate change is occurring on a global scale and may already be responsible for the recent increase in extreme weather events, much of the risk is in some seemingly remote future several decades hence and beyond timeframes relevant for investment purposes. In contrast with mitigation in the form of energy efficiency improvements, which can immediately reduce costs and contribute to profitability, most efforts to improve climate resilience take the form of risk avoidance and only generate a return if and when an extreme event occurs. Adaptation measures are necessarily specific to time and location; adaptive measures in one location may be useless or even inappropriate in another time and place, e.g., buildings may have to be periodically relocated if sea level rise continues, and switching to more heat-resistant seed types can be effective only up to some temperature limit. Most companies also lack the internal knowledge and capacity to evaluate climate science. They need short- to medium-term projections of localized climate impacts, commensurate with the scale of business activity, from sources they trust and understand. While major efforts to improve short-term forecasts are ongoing, downscaled, short-term forecasts from multiple climate models presently often disagree with respect to some key variables such as changes in precipitation. This has so far been a strong rationale for inaction and business-as-usual. (Hurrell, 2009)

There is also evidence that a consequence of global warming and climate change will be greater climate variability, such that even confidence on conditions during the next decade may not hold for decades thereafter (Hallegatte, 2012). Recognizing the problem too openly may also be seen as support for unwelcome regulation (Agrawala et al, 2011). Consequently, surveys show that most businesses perceive consideration of climate risk in their investments and business plans to be unnecessary, technically difficult, and perhaps premature; acknowledging empirical evidence of climate impacts and economic losses can be seen as politically sensitive.

In addition to the lack of reliable climate projections at the scale of a business activity, private companies face several additional obstacles in developing countries. In some countries, access to weather and climate information is limited and tightly controlled by governments and only available for a fee, which can add substantial costs. Companies may also find that they have few short-term options to reduce their risks, or that much of what could be done is within the realm of governments (e.g., improving storm warning systems). When actions have been identified, they may involve trade-offs with short-term profitability (changes in seed varieties), require costly infrastructure (building coastal fortifications), or be difficult to finance.

Misleading but widely held perceptions are that climate change is still unproven and a future rather than current risk, and that adaptation is largely dependent on uncertain model results. There is an erroneous perception among many companies that climate change is primarily an environmental rather than a development issue. The political process, including the climate convention and negotiating process, is notably lacking input from private sector perspectives.

Overcoming the Barriers

Several ways have been proposed, and in a few instances implemented, to address some of these barriers. For certain purposes the most effective response will be regulatory mandates such as building codes and zoning restrictions which directly address the need for cost-effective improvements in building design and location (see below). Lenders and insurers can reinforce or sometimes substitute for regulation through their requirements, viz, refusing to lend or insure buildings that fail to incorporate climate resilience. Investor awareness could also become a significant positive force—assuming metrics and reporting allow informed comparison of climate risks.

For some short-term purposes, such as utility planning for summer and winter peak demand, the most effective method currently available is an assessment of short-term trends (e.g., the past decade) used as a proxy into the future (Miller and Stenek, 2012). A more generally applicable approach goes by various labels, among them "robust decision-making" (Lempert et al, 2004). This concept begins with an assessment of financial vulnerabilities and then evaluates the costs and benefits of options to mitigate the risk, based on estimates of the probability that an event may occur within a given time frame (IFC, 2011a, 2011b, 2011c). For example, a small incremental investment (e.g., increasing the level of a roadbed when building a railroad) may be justified if the probability of extreme flooding due to climate change is one in 20 years but not one in 500 years. Thinking about risks and potential adaptation strategies may also be useful insofar as it informs business management about new risks and opportunities. Companies may also identify needs for greater collaboration with public agencies, e.g., warmer temperatures in some regions may lead to a greater incidence in malarial mosquitoes, which public health agencies could help identify and address.

For some short-term purposes, such as utility planning for summer and winter peak demand, the most effective method currently available is an assessment of short-term trends (e.g., the past decade) used as a proxy into the future (Miller and Stenek, 2012). A more generally applicable approach goes by various labels, among them "robust decision-making" (Lempert et al, 2004). This concept begins with an assessment of financial vulnerabilities and then evaluates the costs and benefits of options to mitigate the risk, based on estimates of the probability that an event may occur within a given time frame (IFC, 2011a, 2011b, 2011c). For example, a small incremental investment (e.g., increasing the level of a roadbed when building a railroad) may be justified if the probability of extreme flooding due to climate change is one in 20 years but not one in 500 years. Thinking about risks and potential adaptation strategies may also be useful insofar as it informs business management about new risks and opportunities. Companies may also identify needs for greater collaboration with public agencies, e.g., warmer temperatures in some regions may lead to a greater incidence in malarial mosquitoes, which public health agencies could help identify and address.

Climate finance can be used to demonstrate and foster private sector understanding and adoption of good adaptation practices. In some sectors, particularly agriculture, there is an emerging appreciation that climate resilience can be a source of competitive advantage, e.g., through the adoption of crop insurance and more robust seed varieties. As a recent UN report describes, this perception can create new market opportunities, especially in emerging markets (UNISDR, 2013).

Successful Early Efforts to Engage the Private Sector in Climate Change Adaptation

International development organizations have begun to address the link between private investment and adaptation in several ways. First steps in this regard have been achieved through projects and programs financed by the Least Developed Countries Fund (LDCF) and the Special Climate Change Fund (SCCF), two funds that were established by the Conference of the Parties (COP) to the United Nations Framework Convention on Climate Change (UNFCCC) in 2001. These funds, managed by the Global Environment Facility (GEF), were established to finance concrete adaptation actions in developing countries. They currently total about $900 million of voluntary contributions from donor countries, and finance adaptation investments mostly through public channels. The LDCF and SCCF operate in cooperation with the regional banks and several UN agencies (for a list of all 10 agencies, see www.thegef.org).

An analysis of the LDCF/SCCF-financed project portfolio implemented by the United Nations Development Programme

(UNDP) shows that the private sector engagement in the portfolio takes place in five ways. Some examples of these five approaches from the GEF UNDP portfolio include:

- **Awareness raising, including potential risks and response measures:** An LDCF project in Cape Verde raised awareness of climate risk, vulnerability and adaptation in the water sector. Weather and climate data have been made more accessible to both policymakers and the private sector, and investments in water capture, storage and distribution have been modified to include adaptation measures.

- **Capacity building to train private entities how to manage climate change risks:** In Sierra Leone, the capacity of more than 50 water engineers from the public and private sectors was enhanced through designing and managing climate risks on small-scale water supply systems and maintaining climate-resilient infrastructure. In Guinea-Bissau, a national multi-sectoral committee, including government, development partners, the private sector, academia and the media, was established to advise on climate change adaptation practices at all levels.

- **Activities that change regulation, policies and institutional infrastructure:** In Zimbabwe, an SCCF project financed the development and implementation of regulatory and fiscal incentives to stimulate climate risk reduction by the private sector and rural households. In Liberia, regulations were introduced on coastal development activities taking into account climate change considerations.

- **Public-private partnerships and efforts that promote private sector responses to climate change:** In Sierra Leone, the LDCF financed a Public Private Sector Forum focused on policies and the promotion of investment and entrepreneurship for managing climate change risks to water distribution and usage. Affordable climate-resilient community-based water harvesting, storage and distribution systems were designed, built and rehabilitated in Freetown, with private sector participation, to withstand projected changes in rainfall patterns and intensity.

- **Entrepreneurship development/encouragement that opens new private sector opportunities for reducing climate vulnerability:** In Samoa, an LDCF project aimed at increasing the resilience of the tourism sector incorporates climate risks into tourism-related policy processes and investments in coastal areas. In South Africa, an SCCF-financed project supported the development of a fire and insurance program, including the establishment of a fire and insurance working group with the involvement of the insurance industry. In Tajikistan, an SCCF project supports the commercialization of climate resilient products through marketing campaign, crop certification, and funding for start-up initiatives and small and medium enterprises by micro-finance institutions and business advisory centers to bring climate resilient products to the market. In Djibouti, an LDCF supported adaptation-oriented micro-finance project supports shade garden-based agro-pastoral enterprises in the Grand and Petit Bara plains.

GEF adaptation initiatives with other partners include an SCCF project in Jordan in collaboration with the International Fund for Agricultural Development utilizing a new irrigation technology that allows water savings of up to 70 percent in drought-prone areas. In Eastern Europe, an SCCF insurance project implemented by the World Bank with locally licensed private insurance companies will enable catastrophe and weather risk insurance policies.

Another source of donor funding for private sector adaptation efforts is the Pilot Program on Climate Resilience, one of several funds that comprise the Climate Investment Funds (www. climateinvestmentfunds.org). The Pilot Program began in 2008 and has mobilized about $1.1 billion to nine countries and two regions chosen for their vulnerability to pilot and demonstrate ways to integrate climate risk and resilience into core development planning.

Several international financial institutions are developing or already applying risk screening tools during their project appraisal. The International Finance Corporation (IFC)'s Performance Standards on Environmental and Social Sustainability, as recently revised, require consideration of climate risks and include guidance on the identification of potential direct and indirect climate-related adverse effects, and definition of monitoring and adaptation measures (WB IEG, 2012). IFC has initiated a process to pilot climate risk screening tools for its investments in the near future (WBG IEG, 2012). The Asia Development Bank has also reported its efforts to develop and apply a climate risk screening process to its investments (UNFCC, 2012).

Actions Needed to Engage the Private Sector in Developing Country Adaptation Efforts

The process of private sector recognition and response to climate change risks has several levels. Businesses must develop a more detailed assessment of the current and potential impacts of climate change, for the location and time horizon relevant to the business. Adaptation measures must be identified and implemented, and must include risk prevention, risk awareness, and perceived risk. There are also economic and regulatory barriers that often discourage or even prevent implementing adaptation measures, as discussed above.

Specifically, there are three primary actions that are required for the private sector to become more fully engaged and effective in responding to climate change in developing countries: Increase awareness about the significance of climate change and the need for responses to it, include the private sector in national and international adaptation efforts, and engage the private sector in developing products and services to reduce costs and impacts of climate change.

Increase awareness about the significance of climate change

As stated earlier, a recent OECD survey suggests that only a minority of respondent businesses have conducted risk assessments and fewer still have evaluated adaptation options. Private sector awareness of the need to respond climate change must start with increased awareness of its significance, potential risks, and necessary response measures. Private companies must realize that climate change is happening, and its consequences may affect them.

An OECD study (Agrawala et al, 2011) found that companies are aware of the gradual and extreme changes in weather events threatened by climate change, but tend to focus more on extreme events rather than gradual changes. They are not fully aware of potential reputational and litigation risks to their businesses. The level of awareness of the potential impacts of climate change on companies and their operations greatly varies. While most companies surveyed recognized current and future risks that climate change may post to their operations, fewer engaged in supplementary activities related to awareness.

The study also found that the levels of engagement of companies at the national and international level appeared to depend on the level of engagement of the public sector, and the public attention given to adaptation to climate change. The private sector may also be influenced by approaches or guidelines suggested by national adaptation strategies or National Adaptation Programmes of Action (NAPAs).

Private sector initiatives to raise climate change awareness may be influenced by input and assistance from international organizations and partnerships. Partnerships with international organizations can help encourage private sector engagement in climate change and adaptation. For example, the United Nations Environment Programme's Finance Initiative Climate Change Working Group has coordinated several financial organizations to promote their engagement in adaptation to climate change, and has worked to understand the climate information requirements of companies in the financial sector as part of their adaptation strategies.

Include the private sector in national and international adaptation efforts

There are multiple ways governments can facilitate private sector adaptation efforts to the benefit of the larger public through provision of information, adoption of sensible regulations, and creation of appropriate economic incentives. This topic was explored and supported at a recent OECD workshop bringing together public and private sector representatives (OECD, 2012c).

One of the most immediate and developmentally important opportunities is with respect to upgrading and achieving financial sustainability for the weather and climate services in developing countries, particularly the poorest and most vulnerable. These agencies often view weather information as a valuable commodity to be protected and sold, which not only limits public access to timely data for farming and other business purposes but also typically creates a lose-lose result: the agency generates very little revenue, and cannot maintain even minimal services (World Bank et al, 2012). Public-private partnerships that help manage and disseminate the climate information could help enable countries to share the rights to weather data and the responsibilities for its management. One option is shared revenue arrangements in which private weather systems maintain systems, help identify customers (e.g., from utilities and other companies with weather information needs), and share some revenue with the appropriate agency. The ultimate goal of such arrangements is to ensure that weather and climate networks are maintained with the highest degree of reliability for the general public and institutional end-users, while reducing the total cost for the developing country.

For example, IFC and the European Bank for Reconstruction and Development are working with the government of Turkey on ways such arrangements could support greater private sector awareness and preparedness for climate change. In collaboration with Turkey's Ministry of Environment and Urbanization and the Union of Chambers and Commodity Exchanges of Turkey, these organizations will manage a year-long market study designed to give the private sector new tools to help anticipate and respond to the effects of climate change. The initiative will work with large and small Turkish businesses to address needs for achieving climate resilience in the private sector (IFC and EBRD, 2011).

As estimates of the financial needs for adapting to climate change rise, the need to identify additional sources of financing also points to the much larger financial resources under private control. There are several reasons to focus on private sector financing of adaptation. One is the need to identify additional sources of funds to complement and enhance the effectiveness of donor funding. The UNFCCC Green Climate Fund noted above commits donor nations to mobilize $100 billion a year in "new and additional" resources for climate change mitigation and adaptation by 2020 from a combination of public and private sources (UNFCCC, 2011). Obtaining this amount from traditional commitments of bilateral and multilateral aid is very unlikely and other sources will need to be found (OECD, 2012b).

Attracting private investment to climate change mitigation and adaptation has thus become part of the discussion of "resource mobilization," one of the primary issues within the climate convention. A closely related issue is the potential for private sector access to climate finance as limited public funds could be used to reduce risks and leverage much greater private investment in climate projects (IFC, 2011a, 2011b, 2011c). The Green Climate Fund provides for a Private Sector Facility, although almost entirely without definition (WRI, 2012).

Engage the private sector in developing products and services to reduce costs and impacts of climate change

The increasing awareness of climate risks represents a business opportunity to develop products and services to increase climate resilience. Many of the needs identified in the NAPAs and other analyses of climate risks and adaptation priorities in developing countries are for products and services that could be provided in the most efficient and sustainable way through cooperation with the private sector. The private sector role may vary from sector to sector and country to country and could take many different forms, from simply serving as a provider of technology to working in partnership with governments to the assumption of primary responsibility for the delivery of adaptation services.

One of the highest priorities identified in the NAPAs and other national adaptation plans is the development of regional weather and climate networks for real-time observation, local-level forecasting, and the dissemination of information. At a time when climate change is threatening the most vulnerable communities, this infrastructure is essential in helping the most vulnerable countries anticipate and communicate early warnings for severe weather events, improve food security and agricultural production, and better manage scarce and dwindling water resources. A viable opportunity for private sector involvement includes the deployment of a network of automated surface weather and climate observation points, which can be used to provide the critical weather information necessary for early warning of severe weather.

The availability of low cost, high quality cellular phone service and remotely communicated weather information is making it possible to provide earlier warnings of storms and extreme weather events. This is possible due to large investments and transfer of technology by private firms, even in many poor countries and remote regions. Climate observation and forecasting, when combined with tailored applications for industries and the public, can be used at the national level to enhance agricultural production, water resource management, and renewable energy. The GEF LDCF Council approved a $50 million grant for 11 projects in May 2012 to deploy such systems in least developed countries. These projects are designed in a flexible manner to allow different options to access, process and disseminate the climate data. One option is to establish public private partnerships to enable local private companies to share the rights to the data and the responsibility for their management.

In addition to the deployment of systems to collect climate information, there is considerable potential for tailoring the existing smart phone and mobile phone markets, which are rapidly growing in developing countries, for real-time communication on extreme weather events (OECD, 2012b). The mobile phone market highlights the potential for private sector-led investments that "leap frog" technologies and provide better services at lower cost than those developed previously.

Arguably a current major omission is the absence of any focused international effort to define and promote technologies of specific benefit for enhancing climate resilience. Many relevant products are appearing in the market such as technologies for desalinization, buildings resistant to high winds, and seeds with greater tolerance for droughts and high temperatures. However, these products are being developed in response to current market demand with little if any expectation of their added value in meeting greater future needs; the return on investment remains too uncertain to justify private risk-taking. One exception may be the research program of the Consultative Group on International Agricultural Research (CGIAR), which includes climate change as an explicit factor guiding some of its research agenda (CGIAR, 2013).

A major issue will be the availability of funding for new adaptation technologies. Support for new climate mitigation technologies has a mixed record, with few initial successes in the GEF program for commercialization of early stage clean energy technologies (Miller, 2007). The Clean Technology Fund, part of the Climate Investment Funds, a multi-donor, multilateral trust fund, allows for subsidized loans to private companies attempting to commercialize new energy technologies. The guidelines for concessional funding (near zero interest credits with a grant element of 75 percent) under the Pilot Program for Climate Resilience refer to funding for "innovation and dissemination of drought tolerant crop varieties," use of biotechnology, and more generally "the additional costs associated with being among the first players to implement a project in a given sector, under new regulations or work through unprecedented systems." (Climate Investment Funds, 2011)

[...]

Conclusion

Engaging the business community in climate change risk, response, and adaptation needs to be a much higher priority in developing countries. Private sector companies should integrate adaptation into their strategies and investments for several reasons:

- First, for *their* economic interest. Many of their investments in development sectors are at risk; therefore, integrating adaptation planning and measures will make their investments and returns less risky and ultimately more profitable.

- Second, but equally important, for their *clients'* interest. Without adaptation measures, most development investments in vulnerable countries are not sustainable. In addition to the economic argument, the ethical imperative for sustainable investment and business practice must also be considered.

- Third, to support the interests of their *countries* of operation. The private sector must become an active partner in adaptation efforts in developing countries as they can bolster governments, help define and complement effective public adaptation measures, and build public and international support through their influence. Although there is an emerging business voice, it needs to be more vocal and effective.

There are several opportunities that companies should take advantage of through early actions on climate change adaptation and climate resilience:

- Developing the tools and methods for risk assessment and risk management is already relatively advanced but

The Paris Agreement

United Nations Framework Convention on Climate Change
The Paris Agreement, which was adopted by 195 countries at the Paris Climate Conference in December of 2015, sets out a global action plan to put the world on track to avoid dangerous climate change by limiting global warming. It is a bridge between today's policies and the goal of climate-neutrality before the end of the century. The following is an excerpt from the agreement.

Paris Agreement
The Parties to this Agreement,
Being Parties to the United Nations Framework Convention on Climate Change, hereinafter referred to as "the Convention,"
Pursuant to the Durban Platform for Enhanced Action established by decision 1/CP.17 of the Conference of the Parties to the Convention at its seventeenth session,
In pursuit of the objective of the Convention, and being guided by its principles, including the principle of equity and common but differentiated responsibilities and respective capabilities, in the light of different national circumstances,
Recognizing the need for an effective and progressive response to the urgent threat of climate change on the basis of the best available scientific knowledge,
Also recognizing the specific needs and special circumstances of developing country Parties, especially those that are particularly vulnerable to the adverse effects of climate change, as provided for in the Convention,
Taking full account of the specific needs and special situations of the least developed countries with regard to funding and transfer of technology,
Recognizing that Parties may be affected not only by climate change, but also by the impacts of the measures taken in response to it,
Emphasizing the intrinsic relationship that climate change actions, responses and impacts have with equitable access to sustainable development and eradication of poverty,
Recognizing the fundamental priority of safeguarding food security and ending hunger, and the particular vulnerabilities of food production systems to the adverse impacts of climate change,

Taking into account the imperatives of a just transition of the workforce and the creation of decent work and quality jobs in accordance with nationally defined development priorities,

Acknowledging that climate change is a common concern of humankind, Parties should, when taking action to address climate change, respect, promote and consider their respective obligations on human rights, the right to health, the rights of indigenous peoples, local communities, migrants, children, persons with disabilities and people in vulnerable situations and the right to development, as well as gender equality, empowerment of women and intergenerational equity,

Recognizing the importance of the conservation and enhancement, as appropriate, of sinks and reservoirs of the greenhouse gases referred to in the Convention,

Noting the importance of ensuring the integrity of all ecosystems, including oceans, and the protection of biodiversity, recognized by some cultures as Mother Earth, and noting the importance for some of the concept of "climate justice," when taking action to address climate change,

Affirming the importance of education, training, public awareness, public participation, public access to information and cooperation at all levels on the matters addressed in this Agreement,

Recognizing the importance of the engagements of all levels of government and various actors, in accordance with respective national legislations of Parties, in addressing climate change.

Also recognizing that sustainable lifestyles and sustainable patterns of consumption and production, with developed country Parties taking the lead, play an important role in addressing climate change.

rarely practiced. It needs to be recognized and promoted by investors, and become standard or expected in business planning.

- Stronger public-private partnerships will be an important vehicle to enhance climate resilience and at the same time, create business opportunities, as is the case with the collection and use of climate data and deployment of early warning system technologies.

- Private firms will develop many of the products and services that will enable lower costs and more effective responses to climate change and can be the basis for growing, profitable businesses.

In closing, a robust involvement of the private sector in managing climate risks in developing countries will bring resilience to vulnerable communities as well as systematic long term sustainability to private investments. Ultimately what is required is no less than a paradigm shift in business thinking toward natural disasters—as a recent UN report termed it, from "shared risk" to "shared value."

Embedding disaster risk management in business processes is increasingly seen as a key to resilience, competitiveness and sustainability—**a business survival kit** in an increasingly unpredictable world. (UNISDR, 2013)

References

Acclimatise, 2009. Carbon Disclosure Project Report 2008; FTSE 350; Building Business Resilience to Inevitable Climate Change. Nottinghamshire, UK. https://www.cdproject .net/CDPResults/65_329_211_Acclimatise_CDP6_FTSE_350_Building_Business_ Resilience_HR%20(2).pdf

Agrawala, S., Hallegatte, S., Shah, A., Lempert, R., Brown, C. & Gill, S., 2011. Private Sector Engagement in Adaptation to Climate Change: Approaches to Managing Climate Risks. OECD Environment Working Papers, No. 39, OECD Publishing. Paris, France. http://dx.doi.org/10.1787/5kg221jkf1g7-en

Atteridge, A. (2011). *Will private finance support climate change adaptation in developing countries?* Stockholm Environment Institute Working Paper, Stockholm, Sweden. Retrieved from http://www.sei-international.org/mediamanager/documents /Publications/SEI-WorkingPaper-Atteridge-WillPrivate FinanceSupportClimate ChangeAdaptationInDeveloping Countries-2011.pdf

Bloomberg. (2013). Investors demand climate-risk disclosure in 2013 proxies. Retrieved February 25, 2013 from http://www.bloomberg.com/news/2013-02-25/investors -demandclimate-risk-disclosure-in-2013-proxies.html

Buchner, B., Falconer, A., Herve´-Mignucci, M., & Trabacchi, C. (2012). The Landscape of Climate Finance 2012. Venice, Italy. Retrieved from http://climatepolicyinitiative.org /wpcontent/uploads/2012/12/The-Landscape-of-Climate-Finance-2012.pdf

Ceres, May 2012. Physical Risks from Climate Change: A Guide for Companies and Investors on Disclosure and Management of Climate Impacts. Boston, MA. http://www.ceres.org/resources/reports/physical-risks-from-climate-change/view.

Ceres, March 2013. Insurer Climate Risk Disclosure Survey 2012. http://www.ceres.org /resources/reports/naic-report/view

CGIAR, Climate Change, Agriculture and Food Security, 2013. http://ccafs.cgiar.org

Climate Investment Funds, 2011. The Use of Concessional Finance in the PPCR. Washington, D.C. http://www.climateinvestmentfunds.org/cif/sites/climateinvestmentfunds .org/files/PPCR%20_Use_of_concessional_finance_in_the_ppcr.pdf

Connell, R., Miller, A., and Stenek, V., 2009. Evaluating the Private Sector Perspective on the Financial Risks of Climate Change. West-Northwest Law Journal, 15:133-148.

Hallegatte, S., Shah, A., Lempert, R., Brown, C., & Gill, S.l, 2012. Investment Decision Making Under Deep Uncertainty—Application to Climate Change. World Bank Policy Research Working Paper. Washington, D.C. http://elibrary.worldbank.org/content /workingpaper/10.1596/1813-9450-6193

Hazell, P., Anderson, J., Balzer, N., Hastrup Clemmensen, A.,, Hess, U., & Rispol, F., 2010. The Potential for Scale and Sustainability in Weather Index Insurance for Agriculture and Rural Livelihoods. International Fund for Agricultural Development and World Food Programme. Rome, Italy.

Hurrell, J., 2009. Decadal Climate Prediction: Challenges and Opportunities. IOP Conference Series: Earth and Environmental Science 6. http://iopscience.iop.org/1755-1315/6/2/022001

IFC, 2011a. Climate Finance: Engaging the Private Sector; A background paper for "Mobilizing Climate Finance," a report prepared at the request of G20 Finance Ministers. Washington, D.C. http://www1.ifc.org/wps/wcm/connect/5d659a804b28afee9978f908d0338960 /ClimateFinance_G20Report.pdf?MOD=AJPERES

IFC, 2011b. Climate Risk and Business; Climate Risk and Financial Institutions. www.ifc .org/climaterisks

IFC, 2011c. Climate Risk and Business: Ports. Washington, D.C. http://www1.ifc.org /wps/wcm/connect/topics_ext_content/ifc_external_corporate_site/ifc+sustainability /publications/publications_report_climateriskandbusiness-ports__wci__1319578898769

IFC, European Bank for Reconstruction and Development, 2011. IFC, EBRD Conduct Market Study in Turkey to Help Businesses Adapt to Climate Change. http://www.ifc.org/IFCExt/Pressroom/IFCPressRoom .nsf/0/8BC090E741C47A9E85257920004883FE

Lempert, R., Nakicenovic, N., Sarewitz, D., & Schlesinger, M.et al, 2004. Characterizing Climate Change Uncertainties for Decision-Makers. Climate Change, 65:1-9.

McHale, C., & Leuirg, S. (2012). Stormy future for U.S. property/casualty insurers: The growing costs and risks of extreme weather events (a Ceres Report). Boston, MA: Ceres. Retrieved from http://www.ceres.org/resources/reports/stormy-future/view

Miller, A., 2007. The Global Environment Facility Program to Commercialize New Energy Technologies. Energy for Sustainable Development, Volume XI, No. 1.

Miller, A., and Stenek, V., May 2012. World Bank: Development in a Changing Climate. A New "Climate Normal" Needed. http://blogs.worldbank.org/climatechange/new-climate -normal-needed

Munich Re, 2012. North America Most Affected by increase in weather-related natural catastrophes (press release, Oct. 17, 2012). http://www.munichre.com/en/media_relations /press_releases/2012/2012_10_17_press_release.aspx

OECD, 2012a. Development: Aid to developing countries falls because of global recession. http://www.oecd.org/document/3/0,3746,en_2649_37413_50058883_1_1_1_37413,00.html

OECD, 2012b. ICTs, the Environment, and Climate Change. http://www.oecd.org/sti/ict/ green-ict

OECD, 2012c. Policy Forum on Adaptation to Climate Change in OECD Countries, Summary Note, 10-11 May 2012. http://www.oecd.org/env/cc/OECD%20Adaptation%20 Policy%20Forum%2010-11%20May%202012%20-%20Summary%20Note.pdf

Extreme Weather Events

Oxfam, 2012. R4 Rural Resilience Initiative; Quarterly Report. http://www.oxfamamerica
.org/publications/r4-rural-resilience-initiative-1
Oxfam, Calvert Investments, Ceres, May 2012. Physical Risks from Climate Change; A
guide for companies and investors on disclosure and management of climate impacts. http://
www.calvert.com/NRC/literature/documents/sr_Physical-Risks-from-Climate-Change.pdf
Porter, E., 2013. "For Insurers, No Doubts on Climate Change," New York Times, May 14,
2013. http://mobile.nytimes.com/2013/05/15/business/insurers-stray-from-the
-conservative-line-on-climate-change.html
Schalatek, L., & Nakhooda, S. (2012). The Green Climate Fund (Climate Finance
Fundamentals Paper 11, Heinrich Boll Stiftung North America). London: ODI and HBF.
Retrieved from: http://www.odi.org.uk/sites/odi.org.uk/files/odi-assets/publications
-opinion-files/7918.pdf
Shorter, G., May 2012. SEC Climate Change Disclosure Guidance: An Overview and
Congressional Concerns. Congressional Research Service. Washington, D.C. http://www
.fas.org/sgp/crs/misc/R42544.pdf
Technology Review, August, 2011. The Cause of Riots and the Price of Food, Technology
Review. http://www.technologyreview.com/view/425019/the-cause-of-riots-and-the
-price-of-food/
United Nations Framework Convention on Climate Change (UNFCCC), 2011. Report of
the Conference of the Parties on its sixteenth session, held in Cancun from 29 November
to 10 December 2010. Decision 1/CP, Paragraph 18. http://unfccc.int/resource/docs/2010
/cop16/eng/07a01.pdf
United Nations Framework Convention on Climate Change (UNFCCC), 2012.
Compendium on methods and tools to evaluate impacts of, and vulnerability and
adaptation to, climate change http://unfccc.int/adaptation/nairobi_work_programme
/knowledge_resources_and_publications/items/5465.php
United Nations Office for Disaster Risk Reduction (UNISDR), 2013. Global Assessment
Report on Disaster Risk Reduction; From Shared Risk to Shared Value: the Business Case
for Disaster Risk Reduction. http://www.preventionweb.net/english/hyogo/gar/2013/en/
home/download.html
Venugopal, S., & Srivastava, A. (2012). Moving the Fulcrum: A primer on public climate
financing instruments used to leverage private capital (World Resources Institute Working
Paper). Washington, DC. Retrieved from ttp://pdf.wri.org/moving_the_fulcrum.pdf
World Bank, 2013. Agriculture, value added (% of GDP) http://data.worldbank.org
/indicator/NV.AGR.TOTL.ZS
World Bank, World Development Report 2010: Development and Climate Change.
Washington, D.C.: World Bank
World Bank Global Facility for Disaster Reduction and Recovery, 2012. Thai Flood 2011:
Rapid Assessment for Resilient Recovery and Reconstruction Planning. Bangkok, Thailand.
https://www.gfdrr.org/gfdrr/sites/gfdrr.org/files/publication/Thai_Flood_2011_2.pdf.
World Bank Internal Evaluation Group, 2012. Adapting to Climate Change: Assessing
World Bank Group Experience. Washington, D.C. http://ieg.worldbankgroup.org/content
/ieg/en/home/reports/climate_change3.html
World Bank, United Nations International Strategy for Disaster Reduction, and World
Meteorological Organization. March, 2012. The Role of Hydrometeorological Services
in Disaster Risk Management: Proceedings from the joint workshop. Washington, D.C.
http://www.gfdrr.org/gfdrr/sites/gfdrr.org/files/The_Role_of_Hydrometeorological_
Services_in_Disaster_Risk_Management_2012.pdf
WRI Insights, August, 2012. What's Next For the Green Climate Fund? http://insights.wri
.org/news/2012/08/whats-next-green-climate-fund

Europe Must Adapt to Climate Change

European Environment Agency

An agency of the European Union, the European Environment Agency (EEA) provides logical and unbiased reporting on the environment. In this article, the EEA—a major information source for those developing and evaluating environmental policy, as well as the general public—discusses how Europe needs to move forward with strategies to combat climate change as extreme weather events continue.

As you read, consider the following questions:

1. What extreme weather events are nations in Europe facing?
2. How can the continent become more resilient as climate change impact worsens?
3. What is the potential cost of ignoring climate change warning signs?

Climate change is causing a variety of impacts to our health, ecosystems and economy. These impacts are likely to become more serious in the coming decades. If not addressed, these impacts could prove very costly, in terms of ill health, adverse effects on ecosystems, and damaged property and infrastructure. Many adaptation projects are already underway across Europe to prepare for a changing climate.

2014 will be remembered across Europe for its extreme weather events. In May 2014, a low-pressure cyclone hit south-eastern Europe, causing widespread flooding and 2,000 landslides across the Balkans. Then in early June 2014, a series of heavy rainstorms hit northern Europe. By July 2014, Europe was suffering from another problem: heat. Eastern Europe and the UK experienced a heatwave.

Extreme weather events as well as gradual changes in the climate—such as rising sea levels and warming oceans—will continue. In fact, these events are expected to become more frequent and more intense in the future. Even if all countries were to radically cut their emissions of greenhouse gases today, the greenhouse gases that have already been released into the atmosphere would continue to have a warming effect on the climate. In addition to substantially reducing greenhouse-gas emissions, countries in Europe and across the world need to put in place policies and measures to adapt to climate change.

Europe's Climate Is Changing

A changing climate will affect almost every aspect of our lives. Increased intensity and frequency of rainfall in many parts of Europe will mean frequent and serious flooding events, destroying homes and affecting other infrastructure (e.g. transport and energy) in risk areas. Elsewhere in Europe, including in southern Europe, higher temperatures and reduced rainfall will mean that many areas might face droughts. This could create competition between agriculture, industry, and households for scarce water resources. It could also create more heat-related health problems.

Climate change will also affect ecosystems across Europe. Many economic sectors depend on healthy and stable ecosystems to provide a variety of products and services to humans. For example, bees pollinate our crops, while forests help to absorb greenhouse gases. Changes to the balance of species and habitats in ecosystems could have wide-reaching effects. A reduction in rainfall in southern Europe could make it impossible to grow certain crops, while higher temperatures might allow alien invasive species and species that carry diseases to migrate northwards.

Warmer oceans are already forcing various fish species to move northward, which in turn puts further pressure on the fisheries sector. For example, the northward shift in mackerel stocks has exacerbated the already existing problem of overfishing of herring and mackerel in the Northeast Atlantic.

Climate Change Has a Cost

Extreme weather events can result in loss of life, and bring economic and social activity in the affected area to a halt. Substantial funds are often required for rebuilding damaged property and infrastructure. However, most of the damage from extreme weather events in recent decades cannot be attributed to climate change alone. Socio-economic developments, and decisions such as expanding cities towards floodplains, are the main causes of the increased damage. But without adaptation actions, damage costs and other adverse effects are projected to increase as our climate continues to change.

The costs of future climate change are potentially very large. Recent research estimates that without adaptation actions, heat-related deaths could reach about 200,000 per year in Europe by 2100, and the cost of river flood damages could be more than EUR 10 billion a year. In the case of extensive climate change and no adaptation actions, forest fires could affect an area of roughly 800,000 hectares every year. The number of people affected by droughts could also increase by a factor of seven to about 150 million per year, and economic losses due to sea-level rise would more than triple to EUR 42 billion a year.

Although climate change is mostly expected to create costs for society, it may also create a limited number of new opportunities, which often come with new risks. Warmer winters in northern Europe might mean a reduced need for winter heating. On the other hand, warmer summers might increase the energy consumed for cooling. With sea ice melting, Arctic sea lanes might be opened to shipping and thus cut transport costs. But increased shipping might expose the Arctic to pollution and should be regulated to ensure that it is safe and clean.

Whatever the projected impacts are, be it more rain, higher temperatures, or less freshwater, European countries need to adapt their rural landscape, cities, and economy to a changing climate and reduce our vulnerability to climate change.

What Is "Climate Change Adaptation"?

"Adaptation" covers a wide range of activities and policies that seek to prepare societies for a changing climate. When adaptation policies are implemented they can reduce the impacts and damage costs of climate change, and prepare societies to thrive and develop in a changed climate. Some of these actions have a relatively low cost, such as information campaigns on how to stay cool in warm weather or an early-warning system for heatwaves. Other adaptation actions can be very expensive, such as building dykes and coastal defences (such construction measures are often referred as "grey adaptation"), relocating houses out of flood-plains, or expanding retention basins to respond to droughts.

Some adaptation measures involve using natural methods to increase an area's resilience to climate change. Such "green adaptation" actions include restoring sand-dunes to prevent erosion or planting trees on river banks to reduce flooding. The city of Nijmegen in the Netherlands has implemented green adaptation measures of this sort. The Waal River bends and narrows around Nijmegen, causing floods in this coastal city. To prevent the damage from these floods, the city is building a canal, giving the river more room to flow. This also creates new spaces for recreation and for nature.

The Dutch Building with Nature programme is another good example of the combination of grey and green adaptation. It has promoted the restoration of coastal wetlands such as swamps, reedbeds, marshes, and mudflats. These wetland areas help to prevent soil subsidence thanks to the root structures of wetland plants. By preventing soil subsidence at coastal areas, this protects the surrounding area from flooding.

Other adaptation measures consist of using laws, taxes, financial incentives and information campaigns to enhance resilience to climate change (measures knowns as "soft adaptation"). An information campaign in Zaragoza, Spain, made the city's 700,000 inhabitants more aware of the need to use water sparingly to survive the lengthier droughts expected for this semi-arid region. Coupled with control of leakage from the water supply distribution network, the project has almost halved daily water use per person compared with 1980, and the city's total water consumption has fallen by 30% since 1995.

Adaptation in the European Union

The European Union and its Member States are already working on climate change adaptation. In 2013, the European Commission adopted the communication "An EU Strategy on adaptation to climate change," which helps countries plan their adaptation activities. The Strategy also promotes the creation and sharing of knowledge, and aims to enhance resilience in key sectors by using EU funds. More than 20 European countries have already adopted adaptation strategies, outlining initial actions they will take (e.g. vulnerability assessments and research) and how they intend to adapt to a changing climate. However, in terms of concrete action on-the-ground, many countries are still at a very early stage.

An EEA survey of adaptation measures showed that water management is the sector that most countries are prioritising. However, countries also direct resources to providing information to their citizens. For example, as part of its efforts to reduce the spread of insect-borne diseases, the region of Emilia Romagna runs an awareness campaign on the dangers of Lyme disease, dengue, and West Nile disease.

Many countries have created online adaptation-knowledge platforms to facilitate the sharing of transnational, national, and local experiences and good practice. The Climate-ADAPT portal, managed by the European Environment Agency and the European Commission, provides a European platform for sharing such experiences.

Not Adapting Is Not a Viable Option

Extreme weather events and EU policies have placed adaptation policies and measures higher on the political agenda in European countries in recent decades. However, according to a recent survey, many countries are prevented from taking action by a lack of resources such as time, money, or technology. "Uncertainties about the extent of future climate change" and "unclear responsibilities" were also seen as barriers by a large number of countries.

The effects of climate change vary from region to region. Policymakers also face the difficulty of incorporating future changes in wealth, infrastructure, and population into their climate-change adaptation plans. What will an increasingly older and urbanised population need in terms of transport, housing, energy, health services, or simply food production, in a changing climate?

Rather than treating adaptation as a separate policy sphere, adaptation can best be implemented through better integration into every other area of public policy. Within their adaptation strategies, EU countries and the European Union are exploring how they can integrate adaptation concerns into different policy spheres such as agriculture, health, energy, or transport.

Extreme weather events in particular show that not adapting is a very costly decision and is not a viable option in the medium and long term. For example, transport infrastructure is often severely damaged in floods. When movement of people, goods, or services is hindered, the indirect costs to the economy can be many times higher than the direct cost of damaged transport infrastructure.

It is clear that, like many other infrastructure projects, adapting transport infrastructure is costly. It may also be difficult because the transport system involves different groups, from vehicle manufacturers to infrastructure managers to passengers. One cost-efficient solution is to consider adaptation measures when infrastructure is built or renewed, and the EU budget offers different funding opportunities to support infrastructure projects.

An effective solution requires a longer-term and wider perspective with the integration of climate change into different public policies around sustainability. In the case of climate change adaptation, this raises questions about how to build our cities, how to transport people and products, how to supply energy to our homes and factories, how to produce our food, and how to manage our natural environment.

It is also clear that an effective combination of adaptation and mitigation measures can help to ensure that future impacts of climate change are limited, and that when they do come, Europe is better prepared and more resilient.

Periodical and Internet Sources Bibliography

The following articles have been selected to supplement the diverse views presented in this chapter.

Lisa Finneran, "Modernizing Weather Forecasts and Disaster Planning to Save Lives," The World Bank, August 9, 2016. http:// blogs.worldbank.org/voices/modernizing-weather-forecasts-and -disaster-planning-save-lives.

Paul Freeman and Koko Warner, "Vulnerability of Infrastructure to Climate Variability: How Does This Affect Infrastructure Lending Policies?" Disaster Management Facility of The World Bank and the ProVention Consortium, October 2001.

Charis Gresser, "Climate Change: Countries Plan for Unpredictable Weather," *Financial Times* (UK), October 13, 2011. https://www .ft.com/content/561c5308-ef38-11e0-918b-00144feab49a.

Thomas M. Kostigen, "Poor Nations Want U.S. to Pay Reparations for Extreme Weather," *USA Today*, September 12, 2015. http://www .usatoday.com/story/news/world/2015/09/12/kostigen-climate -change-reparations/72014440/v.

Sönke Kreft, David Eckstein, and Inga Melchior, "Global Climate Risk Index 2017," Germanwatch, November 2016. https:// germanwatch.org/de/download/16411.pdf.

Coco Liu, "Typhoons Test China's Vulnerability to Extreme Weather," E&E News, August 20, 2015. http://www.eenews.net/ stories/1060023678.

Monirul Mirza, "Climate Change and Extreme Weather Events: Can Developing Countries Adapt?" *Climate Policy Journal*, May 14, 2003.

Monirul Mirza, "Mainstreaming Climate Change for Extreme Weather Events & Management of Disasters: An Engineering Challenge," EIC Climate Change Technology, IEEE, 2006. http:// ieeexplore.ieee.org/abstract/document/4057385.

Jo-Ellen Parry and Anika Terton, "How Are Vulnerable Countries Adapting to Climate Change?" International Institute for Sustainable Development. http://www.iisd.org/faq/adapting-to-climate-change.

Wageningen University and Research, "Extreme Weather Driving Countries to Adapt to Climate Change," October 14, 2014. https:// www.wur.nl/en/newsarticle/Extreme-weather-driving-countries-to -adapt-to-climate-change.htm.

For Further Discussion

Chapter 1

1. What are some examples of unusually extreme weather around the world?
2. What is the link between ocean levels, temperatures, and extreme weather?

Chapter 2

1. Discuss one example of extreme weather and the specific effect it has had on a place.
2. Why is it important to study the effects of extreme weather on animals as well as humans?

Chapter 3

1. What is the major argument used by those skeptical of global warming?
2. How does human activity cause global warming?

Chapter 4

1. Discuss the historic importance of the Paris Agreement.
2. What are some of the specific things being done by countries around the world to reduce the effects of climate change and extreme weather?

Organizations to Contact

The editors have compiled the following list of organizations concerned with the issues debated in this book. The descriptions are derived from materials provided by the organizations. All have publications or information available for interested readers. The list was compiled on the date of publication of the present volume; the information provided here may change. Be aware that many organizations take several weeks or longer to respond to inquiries, so allow as much time as possible.

American Association for the Advancement of Science
1200 New York Avenue NW
Washington, DC 20005
phone: (202) 326-6400
website: http://www.aaas.org

The AAAS seeks to advance science, engineering, and innovation throughout the world for the benefit of all people. It fosters science education, works to improve communication between scientists, engineers, and the public, and supports science and technology.

Citizens' Climate Lobby
1330 Orange Avenue, #309
Coronado, CA 92118
phone: (619) 437-7142
website: https://citizensclimatelobby.org

Citizens' Climate Lobby is a nonprofit, nonpartisan, grassroots advocacy organization focused on national policies to address climate change.

Climate Action Network International
Rmayl, Nahr Street, Jaara Building, 4th Floor
PO Box: 14-5472
Beirut, Lebanon
website: http://www.climatenetwork.org

The Climate Action Network is a network of nongovernmental organizations working around the world to combat climate change.

The Climate Reality Project
750 9th Street NW
Suite 520
Washington, DC 20001
website: http://www.climaterealityproject.org

The mission of the Climate Reality Project is to unite people all over the world in finding a global solution to the climate crisis by making urgent action a necessity across every level of society.

Earthjustice
50 California Street, Suite 500
San Francisco, CA 94111
phone: (800) 584-6460
website: http://www.earthjustice.org

Earthjustice is a nonprofit public interest law organization based in the United States dedicated to environmental issues.

Environmental Defense Fund
257 Park Avenue South
New York, NY 10010
phone: (800) 684-3322
website: http://www.edf.org

The Environmental Defense Fund's mission is to preserve the natural systems on which all life depends. It works to solve the most critical environmental problems facing the planet in areas that span the biosphere: climate, oceans, ecosystems, and health.

Intergovernmental Panel on Climate Change
c/o World Meteorological Organization
7bis Avenue de la Paix
C.P. 2300
CH-1211 Geneva 2
Switzerland
website: http://www.ipcc.ch

The Intergovernmental Panel on Climate Change (IPCC) is the international body for assessing the science related to climate change. The IPCC was set up in 1988 by the World Meteorological Organization (WMO) and United Nations Environment Programme (UNEP).

Sierra Club
National Headquarters
2101 Webster Street, Suite 1300
Oakland, CA 94612
phone: (415) 977-5500
website: http://www.sierraclub.org

The Sierra Club is the largest and most influential grassroots environmental organization in the United States. Its work includes protecting millions of acres of wilderness and helping pass the Clean Air Act, Clean Water Act, and Endangered Species Act. Currently, it is working to shift energy consumption away from fossil fuels that cause climate disruption and toward a clean energy economy.

Union of Concerned Scientists
Two Brattle Square
Cambridge, MA 02138-3780
phone: (617) 547-5552
website: http://www.ucsusa.org

The Union of Concerned Scientists uses rigorous, independent science to solve the planet's most pressing problems. It combines technical analysis and effective advocacy to create innovative, practical solutions for a healthy, safe, and sustainable future.

United Nations Environment Programme
United Nations Avenue, Gigiri
PO Box 30552, 00100
Nairobi, Kenya
website: http://web.unep.org

The United Nations Environment Programme (UNEP) is the leading global environmental authority that sets the global environmental agenda, promotes the implementation of the environmental dimension of sustainable development within the United Nations system, and serves as an authoritative advocate for the global environment.

World Meteorological Organization
7bis, Avenue de la Paix
Case postale 2300
CH-1211 Geneva 2
Switzerland
website: http://www.wmo.int

WMO is a specialized agency of the United Nations (UN). It is the UN system's authoritative voice on the state and behavior of Earth's atmosphere, its interaction with the land and oceans, the weather and climate it produces, and the resulting distribution of water resources.

Bibliography of Books

Donald C. Ahrens, *Extreme Weather and Climate.* Pacific Grove, CA: Brooks Cole, 2010.

Jeffrey Bennett, *A Global Warming Primer: Answering Your Questions About the Science, the Consequences, and the Solutions.* Big Kid Science, 2016.

Riley E. Dunlap and Robert J. Brulle, *Climate Change and Society: Sociological Perspectives.* New York, NY: Oxford University Press, 2015.

Amitav Ghosh, *The Great Derangement: Climate Change and the Unthinkable.* Chicago, IL: University of Chicago Press, 2016.

Carol Hand, *Climate Change: Our Warming Earth.* Minneapolis, Minnesota: Abdo Publishing, 2015.

Justin Healey, Extreme Weather and Natural Disasters. Thirroul, Australia.: Spinney Press, 2012.

Nick Hunter, *Science vs. Climate Change.* London: Raintree, 2016.

Julia Leyda and Diane Negra, eds., *Extreme Weather and Global Media.* New York, NY: Routledge, 2015.

Michael E. Mann, *The Madhouse Effect: How Climate Change Denial Is Threatening Our Planet, Destroying Our Politics, and Driving Us Crazy.* New York, NY: Columbia University Press, 2016.

George Marshall, *Don't Even Think About It: Why Our Brains Are Wired to Ignore Climate Change.* New York, NY: Bloomsbury Publishing, 2015.

J.R. McNeill, *The Great Acceleration: An Environmental History of the Anthropocene since 1945.* Cambridge, MA: Harvard University Press, 2016.

Patrick J. Michaels and Robert Balling Jr., *Climate of Extremes: Global Warming Science They Don't Want You to Know.* Washington, DC: Cato Institute, 2010.

Michael H. Mogil, *Extreme Weather: Understanding the Science of Hurricanes, Tornadoes, Floods, Heat Waves, Snow Storms, Global Warming, and Other Atmospheric Disturbances.* New York, NY: Black Dog and Leventhal, 2010.

Robert Muir-Wood, *The Cure for Catastrophe: How We Can Stop Manufacturing Natural Disasters.* New York, NY: Basic Books, 2016.

Andrea C. Nakaya, *What Are the Consequences of Climate Change?* San Diego, CA: ReferencePoint Press, 2017.

Roger A. Pielke Jr., *The Rightful Place of Science: Disasters and Climate Change*. Tempe, AZ: Consortium for Science, Policy & Outcomes, 2014.

Joseph Romm, *Climate Change: What Everyone Needs to Know*. New York, NY: Oxford University Press, 2015.

Rebecca Rowell and Venitia Dean, *Weather and Climate Through Infographics*. Minneapolis, MN: Lerner Publications, 2014.

Bonnie Schneider and Max Mayfield, *Extreme Weather: A Guide to Surviving Flash Floods, Severe Snowstorms, Hurricanes, Tsunamis, and Other Natural Disasters*. New York, NY: Palgrave Macmillan, 2012.

Joshua Sneideman, Erin Twamley, and Mike Crosier, *Climate Change: Discover How it Impacts Spaceship Earth*. White River Junction, VT: Nomad Press, 2015.

Adam Sobel, *Storm Surge: Hurricane Sandy, Our Changing Climate, and Extreme Weather of the Past and Future*. New York, NY: Harper Wave, 2014.

Index

A

Africa (eastern), climate
    change and food security
    in, 104–107
air quality, impact of climate
    change on, 83–85, 137
Ait-Chellouche, Youcef, 107
Allen, Myles, 75
animal populations, climate
    change and, 49, 93–102,
    138
Argentina, 73
Atlantic Ocean, 25, 29, 37, 38,
    39
Australia, 18, 21, 59–60,
    72–73, 174

B

Biagini, Bonizella, 202–224
Bloomberg, Michael, 64
Brazil, 48, 145, 147, 148,
    174–175
Burns, Tom R., 181–201
Burundi, 105–106

C

Cambodia, 103
Cameroon, 112
Canada, 18, 49, 75–76, 77, 175
cap-and-trade plans, 174, 178

carbon dioxide, 13, 30, 38,
    40, 41, 44, 51–53, 67, 88,
    109–110, 119–120, 124,
    125, 126–127, 136, 139,
    149, 150, 154, 163, 167,
    168, 169–170
China, 20, 47, 49, 142, 144,
    145, 146, 147–148, 151,
    152, 157, 168, 169, 175–
    176
Clark, Duncan, 154
Clean Air Act, 67
climate change/
    global warming
    and animal populations, 49,
        93–102, 138
    common questions about,
        40–55
    consequences of, 44–55,
        81–92, 104–107, 135–
        140, 227
    definition of, 19
    differentiated responsibility
        for, 141–156
    extreme weather and,
        17–34, 45–49, 64–70,
        71–77, 136–137
    and global health, 81–92
    human causation of, 13–14,
        42, 71–72, 118–134,
        135–136, 139, 162–170
    private sector and, 202–224

Curry, Judith, 167, 168

D

Denchak, Melissa, 135–140
differentiated responsibility for
climate change, 141–156
Dijkgraaf, Robert, 166
disease, vectorborne, increase
in, 53, 86–87, 94, 95–98
Djibouti, 212

E

Eckstein, D., 103
ecosystems, effect of global
warming on, 49–51
Egypt, 112
Emanuel, Kerry, 66, 67, 68
Ethiopia, 106, 112
Europe/European Union
climate change and, 225–231
and meeting emission
reduction goals, 176
and sea level rise, 60–61
European Environment
Agency, 225–231
European heatwave of 2003,
22, 27, 28, 30, 39
European Project on Ocean
Acidification, 52
extreme weather
climate change and, 17–34,
45–49, 64–70, 71–77,
136–137
definition of, 12

and famine, 94, 108–114

F

famine, extreme weather and,
94, 108–114
Francis, Jennifer, 70

G

Gates, Bill, 161
glaciers, 120–121
Global Biodiversity Outlook, 52
greenhouse effect, 41–42, 44,
139
greenhouse gases, 13, 18, 23,
29, 30, 31, 32, 36, 40,
41–42, 44, 46, 50, 51, 67,
113, 123, 125, 139, 141,
143, 144, 145, 157–161,
162, 173–180, 226
Guinea-Bissau, 211
Gulledge, Jay, 17–34

H

Hagen, U., 103
Haiti, 103, 112
Haiyan, Typhoon, 76–77, 158
Haq, Aliya, 136, 137, 140
Helmer, Madeleen, 105
Heming, Julian, 77
Hiebert, Murray, 157–161
Hirschi, Joel, 39
Holdren, John, 76
Honduras, 103
Huber, Daniel, 17–34

hurricanes, 12, 18, 21, 22, 29, 30, 45, 46, 48, 59, 60, 64–70
hydrofluorocarbons, 41

I

India, 22, 103, 111, 142, 144, 145, 146, 147, 148, 151, 152, 157, 158, 168, 169, 177
Indonesia, 112, 125, 158, 159, 177–178
Industrial Revolution, 120, 139, 143
Intergovernmental Panel on Climate Change (IPCC), 71, 72, 77, 93, 103, 128, 138, 162, 164, 165–167, 170
International Federation of Red Cross and Red Crescent Societies, 104–107
Irene, Hurricane, 22

J

Japan, 178
Junghans, L., 103

K

Katrina, Hurricane, 18, 30, 59, 122
Katyunguruza, Anselme, 107
Kerestan, C., 103
Khor, Martin, 149, 150
Knutson, Tom, 67, 68, 69
Kreft, S., 103

Kyoto Protocol, 142, 143, 147, 149, 152, 153, 173, 174, 175, 176, 177, 178

L

Landsea, Christopher, 67–68
Leahy, Stephen, 47
Liberia, 211
Lindzen, Richard, 118
Lubroth, Juan, 93–102

M

Machado Des Johansson, Nora, 181–201
Malaysia, 158
Mandia, Scott, 43
Marsh, Robert, 39
McQuaid, John, 64–70
methane, 13, 41, 125, 136, 163, 169–170
Mexico, 112, 147, 148
Miller, Alan, 202–224
Morocco, 112
Muller, Richard, 131
Munich Re, 18
Myanmar, 103, 160

N

Nargis, Cyclone, 160
National Climate Assessment, 135
National Oceanic and Atmospheric Administration, 44, 48, 49,

66, 67, 68, 73, 131, 136
Netherlands, 28, 60–61, 62
nitrous oxide, 41
NPR, 173–180

O

Obama, Barack, 64
oceans
    climate and, 35–38
    increased acidification of,
        51–53, 138
Ottery, Christine, 71–77
ozone, 50–51, 83–84, 109, 111,
    137

P

Pakistan, 18, 20, 21, 48, 112
Paris Agreement/Paris
    Climate Summit, 57, 103,
    157–161
    text excerpt from, 220–221
perfluorocarbons, 41
pests/vectorborne disease,
    increase in, 53, 86–87, 94,
    95–98
Philippines, 76–77, 103, 112,
    158–159
Physicians for Social
    Responsibility, 108–114
polar ice caps, 120
Powell, James Lawrence,
    129–130
Prothero, Donald R., 118–134

R

Russia, 18, 20, 22, 31, 47, 73,
    178–179
Rwanda, 106

S

Sabushimike, Jean Marie, 106
Samoa, 212
Sandy, Hurricane, 58, 64, 66,
    70, 77
sea level rise, 13, 51, 69, 94,
    109, 121–122, 138–139,
    164, 190
    effect on coastal cities, 51,
        56–63, 121–122, 139
Senegal, 112
Serreze, Mark, 169
Shah, Anup, 40–55, 141–156
Sierra Leone, 211
snow, global warming and, 29
South Africa, 148, 179, 212
Southeast Asia, and response
    to Paris Climate Summit,
    157–161
Stott, Peter, 73
sulphur hexafluoride, 41
Summers, Larry, 153
super-storms, 46–47
sustainable development,
    and climate change
    adaptation, 181–201
Suurkula, Jaan, 49–51

T

Taalas, Petteri, 13
Tajikistan, 212
Texas drought of 2011, 18, 21, 25
Thailand, 112, 160, 205
Thead, Erin A., 56–63
Thomas, Frank, 162–170
tornadoes, climate change and, 23, 29–30
Trenberth, Kevin, 66, 119
Turkey, 148

U

United Kingdom, 31, 39, 74–75, 148, 154, 226
United Nations Environment Programme, 35–38
United States
    and extreme weather, 20, 21–22, 23, 75–76
    increasing severity of coastal hurricanes, 64–70
    and Kyoto Protocol, 143, 152
    and meeting emission reduction goals, 180
    sea level rise/coastal resilience, 56–63
United States Environmental Protection Agency, 81–92

V

Vietnam, 159–160

W

Ward, Bob, 72
water vapor, 41
World Meteorological Organization (WMO), 13, 44, 45–46, 72
World Wildlife Fund (WWF), 46, 51

Y

Yemen, 112

Z

Zimbabwe, 211